Get Ready...
Get Set...
GROW!

*Church Growth for Town
and Country Congregations*

Gary W. Exman

C.S.S. Publishing Co., Inc.
Lima, Ohio

44 196

GET READY . . . GET SET . . . GROW!

Copyright © 1987 by
The C.S.S. Publishing Company, Inc.
Lima, Ohio

Second Printing 1989

Library of Congress Cataloging-in-Publication Data

Exman, Gary W., 1941-
  Get ready — get set — grow!

  Bibliography: p.
  1. Church growth — United States.   2. Small churches.
3. Rural churches.   4. Church growth — United Methodist
Church (U.S.)   5. United Methodist Church (U.S.)
6. Methodist Church — United States.   I. Title.
BR526.E96   1987   254'.5   86-28363
ISBN 0-89536-865-X

7824 / ISBN 0-89536-865-X   PRINTED IN U.S.A.

Acknowledgements

I wish to thank my wife Juanita for her tireless work and her never-ending encouragement to me. She kept me writing.

Thanks also to my secretary, Shirley Gleim, for her diligent work on behalf of this project.

Dedication

This book is dedicated to my son Jonathan and my daughter Bethany. May they always grow in Him. It is dedicated, also, to the members of the Wheelersburg, Ohio, United Methodist Church, in appreciation for their willingness to apply the principles of Church Growth.

4

Copyrighted Sources Quoted With Permission

Arn, Charles; Arn, Win; and McGavran, Donald. *Growth a New Vision for the Sunday School.* Church Growth Press, 709 E. Colorado, Suite 150, Pasadena, CA. 92202 © 1980. Used by Permission.

Benjamin, Paul. *The Growing Congregation.* Lincoln, Ill.: Lincoln Christian College Press. 1971. Used by Permission.

Boer, Harry R. *Pentecost and Missions.* Lutterworth Press, Cambridge. 1961. Used by Permission.

Dayton, Edward R. And Fraser, David A. *Planning Strategies For World Evangelization.* Grand Rapids: Eerdmans, 1980. Used by Permission.

DeRidder, Richard R. *Discipling the Nations.* Grand Rapids: Baker, 1971. Used by Permission.

Dudley, Carl S. *Making The Small Church Effective.* Nashville: Abingdon, 1978. Used by Permission.

Glasser, Arthur F.; Hiebert, Paul G.; Wagner, C. Peter; and Winter, Ralph D. *Crucial Dimensions in World Evangelism.* Pasadena: William Carey Library, 1705 N. Sierra Bonita Ave., Pasadena, CA 91104 © 1976. Used by Permission.

Hoge, Dean R. *Understanding Church Growth and Decline 1950-1978,* ed. Dean R. Hoge and David A. Roozen. Copyright © 1979, The Pilgrim Press. Used by Permission.

Kelley, Dean M. *Why Conservative Churches Are Growing.* Copyright © 1972 by Dean M. Kelley, Reprinted by permission of Harper & Row Publishers, Inc.

Kromminga, Carol G. *Bringing God's News to Neighbors.* Nutley, N.J.: Presbyterian and Reformed, 1976. Used by Permission.

Mavis, W. Curry. *Advancing the Smaller Church.* Grand Rapids: Baker, 1968. Used by Permission.

McGavran, Donald; Hunter, George G. III. *Church Growth Strategies that Work.* Nashville, Abingdon, 1980. Used by Permission.

McGavran, Donald A. *Ethnic Realities and the Church: Lessons from India.* by Permission of William Carey Library, 1705 N. Sierra Bonita Ave., Pasadena, CA 91104. © 1979. Used by Permission.

McGavran, Donald A. *Understanding Church Growth.* (Wm. B. Eerdmans, 1980). Copyright © 1970 Wm. B. Eerdmans Publishing Co. Used by Permission.

Parker, Percy Livingstone. *The Journal of John Wesley.* Copyright © _____. Moody Press. Moody Bible Institute of Chicago. Used by Permission.

Snyder, Howard. *The Radical Wesley.* Downers Grove, ILL: InterVarsity Press, 1980. Used by Permission.

Sweet, William W. *Methodism in American History.* New York: Abingdon Press, 1953. Used by Permission.

Wagner, C. Peter. *Our Kind of People.* Atlanta: John Knox Press, 1979. Used by Permission of the author.

Wagner, C. Peter. *Your Church Can Grow.* Copyright © 1976. Regal Books, Ventura, CA 93006. Used by Permission.

Wagner, C. Peter. *Your Spiritual Gifts Can Help Your Church Grow.* Copyright © 1979. Regal Books, Ventura, CA 93006. Used by Permission.

Wesley, John. *A Plain Account of Christian Perfection.* London: The Epworth Press, 1952. Used by Permission.

Yoder, John H. *The Challenge of Church Growth: A Symposium,* Wilbert R. Shenk, ed. (Scottdale, Pa.: Herald Press, 1973), pp. 45-46. Used by Permission.

Table of Contents

Foreword

The decade of the eighties is a time of great hope for mainline Christianity. It is a decade which is seeing a turnaround in vitality and growth. A serious decline in membership which has extended to twenty years is being reversed. This is being done through four extremely significant emphases now gaining more prominence on the agendas of the mainline churches:

1. A renewed emphasis on biblical evangelism which follows Jesus' Great Commission and seeks to share the faith and make disciples of unchurched men and women.

2. Planting new churches. Denominational executives are beginning to recognize that the most effective methodology for evangelizing unchurched Americans is to start new churches.

3. Reaching out to America's ethnic minorities. It is now understood that America is not a "melting pot," but rather a "stew pot," in which each ethnic group needs to be evangelized on its own terms.

4. New, turnaround growth patterns in existing churches. Many churches in cities, suburbs, small towns, and rural areas are discovering that nongrowth is a disease, and usually a curable disease. They are taking steps to cure it.

In this exciting new book Gary Exman makes a substantial contribution to the process of reversing church decline in America. He deals in depth with the phenomenon of small town and rural churches, a category which includes a full three-quarters of United Methodist congregations. The percentage will be similar in most of America's mainline Protestant denominations.

The book is important because it is one of very few books which deal with small town and rural churches. There is a growing bibliography on small churches in general, but only a couple other titles which analyze the dynamics of small town and rural churches, and those titles are long since outdated. From this perspective alone, it is a much needed work.

Gary Exman also adds a dimension frequently lacking even in the books on small churches in general. He brings to his study an underlying belief that large numbers of existing small town and rural churches can and should grow. At one point he declares, "God's will is for the church to grow." Such a theological assumption, with which I heartily agree, carries many corollaries which cut across theological presuppositions which have dominated the scene for the past twenty years. I believe that Exman is riding the wave of the future.

Gary Exman is a careful student of church growth principles. He completed a doctoral degree with a concentration in the field. He is one of a growing number of mainline pastor-scholars who are able to contextualize church growth principles for mainline churches. He writes as a United Methodist primarily to the mainline denomination audience. His vocabulary is familiar to the mainline denominations. It is not the perspective of an outsider urging renewal and growth, but the perspective of "one of us."

This is a book of inspiration and hope. There is no intrinsic need for America's second largest Protestant denomination to lose one million members every ten years. Exman is speaking a prophetic word to his fellow Methodists and to other mainline denominations who are losing members. The heirs of Wesley and Asbury and Coke do have a contemporary message for millions of unchurched Americans who will listen to them and respond gladly. Here the passion for reaching them and meeting their deepest needs with the gospel in the Methodist way comes through loud and clear.

It is also a practical book. Much more than a homily or a pep talk, the book tells how to do it. Exman speaks as pastor-to-pastor. His theoretical base is strong, but he moves beyond it to the implementation of the principles on the grassroots level. If every Annual Conference or other judicatory would distribute this book to its small town and rural church leaders, both clergy and lay, hold seminars and symposia on its contents, set realistic goals for congregational growth, and apply Gary Exman's recommendations ruthlessly, church growth patterns all across the country would change for the better.

But this is not a book exclusively for United Methodists. It is a model for all. Pastors and lay readers across the board, regardless of their denominational affiliation, will benefit greatly from reading it and implementing its teachings. I see it as a major contribution to the contemporary literature on pastoral theology and church development in America today.

C. Peter Wagner
Professor of Church Growth
Fuller Theological Seminary

Introduction

The churches are the most diverse in America today. Large gothic-like cathedrals steeped in liturgy and ritual are seen across the land. Besides these huge edifices, literally hundreds of small, rural churches steeped in traditions of simplicity and revivalism can also be seen dotting the land. Yet, each individual group is called the church. The denominations have their unique differences, with liberals at one end of the spectrum and fundamentalists at the other. There is much diversity in tradition and theology.

The typical American community has churches of all sizes. The small towns have some churches of over 1,000 members, but they also have some very small chapels. The rural churches are almost all small in size; only a handful have an average attendance of over one hundred and most would average under seventy-five in attendance.

Although, the bulk of the membership in the American churches comes from the churches in the cities, the small town and rural churches make up over seventy-five percent of the total number of congregations. This means that the small town and rural churches are served by seventy-five percent of the pastors while they serve less than half the members of the church.

Most small town and rural churches were started anywhere from thirty to two hundred years ago by the early pioneers of the faith. In the earliest years, as small communities developed and rural areas became more populated, vigorous evangelists and circuit riders traveled to those areas to hold camp meetings and start churches. Their faithfulness to the spreading of the gospel prevailed and the newly-converted people who became their followers started Sunday church schools and churches in meeting houses and vacant buildings as well as in the new converts' homes. Soon buildings for worship were erected, many of which are the existing houses of worship dotting the American rural and town countryside today. Some of these earlier buildings have been replaced by newer more modern structures in recent years.

I have preached in, led workshops at, or visited over one hundred fifty of these small town and rural churches in the past twenty-one years. I am amazed at the beauty of the church buildings and grounds and the luxury of the worship centers and educational facilities. As

I write, scores of them flash as pictures in my mind. These church buildings exemplify the pride of the people who built them.

I have talked to literally thousands of laymen and ministers over the twenty-one years I have been a minister. The dedication of the leaders and followers of these small town and rural churches is extraordinary. The bulk of these layfolk love their churches and are proud of their individual traditions. I am proud to be one of their ministers because we share such a rich heritage and tradition.

However, as I have checked the individual church records and listened to the talk of these dedicated laypeople and ministers, I have become convinced that a vast majority of these churches are declining in attendance at worship and Sunday church school and declining in membership. This decline has been documented. Statistics indicate the decline is in both membership in church and in Sunday church school.[1] Some of the leaders of the United Methodist denomination predict the church will fold in a few short decades unless the decline is reversed.

Therefore, I find myself part of a dedicated and proud tradition which has a cancer of decline eating away at its center. This cancer is so vicious, the denominations are dying and will not exist in a few short decades unless the decline is reversed. I believe the Church Growth movement can reverse the decline.

As a member of the clergy, therefore, I have written this handbook explaining how to implement Church Growth principles in the ministry of your small town or rural churches. This handbook is a practical presentation of Church Growth principles as applied to our small town and rural churches. The approach is more pragmatic than theological because the theological and biblical truths have already been explained adequately by leading Church Growth advocates such as Wagner, Arn, McGavran, Hunter, and Schaller. There are, however, some extensive discussions of biblical principles in Chapters 1 and 3. Therefore, I submit this handbook to you interested lay persons and clergy who are in small town and rural churches and who want to see those churches grow. A careful study and implementation of these practical principles, written for the understanding of both trained clergy and interested and enthusiastic lay people, will revitalize a local church. I believe the result will be churches which will conquer the cancer of decline from within and once again become vital and growing.

I. An Appeal to Reason

The principles of Church Growth have much to offer small town and rural churches regardless of their size. These principles have already been applied to scores of churches of all denominations across the land, and they have proven themselves effective. In the past few years, some pastors have begun applying the principles of Church Growth to the membership of their existing local churches with rewarding results. Several of these churches have documented remarkable growth in the midst of denominations which are declining in membership. The word from the Church Growth movement is that growth can and will happen when the principles of Church Growth are applied.

Many of these testimonies of growth are in urban and suburban settings. The glowing testimonies of growth are happening where large segments of the American population live and are reachable by these growing churches.

The conviction of this author is that small town and rural churches also can grow. The statistics will not be staggering nor the growth as dramatic, yet small town and rural churches can and will grow when the principles of Church Growth are applied.

I have served small town and rural churches for eighteen of my twenty-one years in the ministry. In my most recent pastorate, the community consisted of 1,200-plus communicants and the vitality of our growing church reached into walks of life and commerce of the community. (See chart on page 146.)

In spite of times of economic difficulty, the town still was in a growth process. Likewise, the church continued to grow and flourish in spite of the difficulties of the times. Yet the other churches in the community were not growing. Why were we growing when the other churches were not? The answer was obvious. We were applying the principles of Church Growth and they were not applying these principles.

Church Growth worked in our church because the church as a whole accepted my leadership in guiding them into the principles of Church Growth programs, as we implemented Church Growth concepts into every fiber of the church's program and life. Our worship attendance grew from an average 145 in 1973 to an average 218 in 1984. Our Sunday church school, which was entering a tailspin of decline in 1973 — and which was almost terminated in 1974 through 1976, was turned around and became a vital, functioning, strong arm of the church's total life. (See chart on page 146.) Our group life, which was insignificant if not non-existent in 1973, became a vital part of the church. By 1984, eight small groups met regularly within the building and out in the community. Our giving quadrupled in twelve years. We built an educational addition which cost $320,000 and in five years, only owed $60,000. We had instituted an annual Missionary Conference which raised an additional $7,000 faith promise mission's money for second mile giving.

These growth programs were just some of our accomplishments. Most important, though, we increased our net membership by one hundred fifty-three members even with the loss of scores of members through death, transfer and withdrawal. This feat was accomplished by a vigorous calling program which we developed and which was highly important to our growth over a nine-year period.

Statistically speaking, we did not sound as impressive as the glory stories which can be told by growing churches in urban and suburban areas. Yet, when all variables were considered and the potential of reachable people was considered, our church had grown substantially. The work we did at Convoy, Ohio, was significant for a study in Church Growth. On the basis of our experience, we can give assurance to other churches in small towns and even rural settings that church growth is possible when the church maps out a strategy for growth by using the principles of Church Growth. It is reasonable to grow churches in the small town and rural setting. The methods were tried — and they work.

II. The Application of History and Tradition

The principles of Church Growth have a backbone in historic Christian movements. The founding father of the Methodist Movement, John Wesley, implemented Church Growth principles within his ministry even though he was not aware of the so-called Church Growth movement during the time of his ministry. Many of the concepts of the Church Growth movement are virtually the same as Wesley's concepts of evangelism and growth.

Martin Luther's call of the people to return to the Scriptures rings true to the concepts of Church Growth. The great Lutheran reform movement guided the church back to basics. The other great Christian reform movements, too, are steeped in what is now known as the modern-day Church Growth movement.

Donald McGavran and Waskom Pickett both researched and studied people movements in India and elsewhere in the early 1930s and 1940s. Donald McGavran said that, following an examination of Waskom Pickett's studies, his own research into Church Growth began.[2] We are just beginning today to pick up where Bishop Pickett and Dr. Donald McGavran began. Thus the history and the tradition of the church is based on principles that were forerunners of what are now called Church Growth principles.

III. The Foundation of Scripture

God's will is for the church to grow. The New Testament injunctions point to vital and growing churches which applied the biblical principles of growth. Scripture points out that growth is essential to the Christian community. Applying these biblical principles can and will make small town and rural churches grow. The first century church was a vital, growing organism. Its growth is recorded in the pages of the Book of the Acts of the Apostles and the New Testament Epistles. We must found our evangelism today upon these same ageless Scriptures. The principles of Church Growth are firmly founded in the scriptural report.

It is time for the church to grow and the small town and rural churches can be at the forefront of that growth. As the principles of Church Growth are applied to these conservative, rural communities and farm lands across America, the inspiration for even greater growth in the urban and suburban settings will be ignited. The fire of church growth will begin and the churches will once again become growing, vital churches through the end of this century and into the beginning of the next. The call to reason, history, tradition, and Scripture is rooted in the principles of Church Growth.

Here, then, is a brief synopsis of what is to come:

• Chapter one discusses the historical appeal of Church Growth principles to the church today. In this chapter we examine the individuals who originated the movement and the historical growth of the movement.

• In Chapter two we examine small town and rural churches distinctives as viewed from the perspective of the church at Ephesus.

• Chapter three is an analysis of the small town and rural churches from their early planting to their growth to 1965. The chapter concludes with a presentation of the unique factors in these churches which determine methods of applying Church Growth principles.

• Chapters four through seven discuss several of the Church Growth principles and their growth application to the small town and rural churches. The Church Growth principles examined are the homogeneous unit principle in Chapter four, the principle of celebration, congregation and cell in Chapter five, the principle of redemption and lift in Chapter six, and the understanding of resistance and receptivity in Chapter seven.

• Finally, Chapter eight outlines a way to develop Church Growth strategy for small town and rural churches. It stresses the importance of a Church Growth pastor, the importance of an inspired laity, the importance of the gift of evangelist and, finally, the implementation of a calling program.

Chapter 1

The Historical Appeal of Church Growth Principles for the Churches of Today

There are many facets of church history which must be understood in order to make the case for Church Growth principles as a valid program for outreach. There are four aspects of significance. The *first* is the history of the Church Growth movement, which includes (a) the input of Bishop Waskom Pickett and (b) the influence of Donald McGavran and the Fuller School. The *second* is the history of the Wesleyan Movement. The *third* is the growth of the United Methodist church in America. The *fourth* is the study of Church Growth principles in the United Methodist Church.

The History of the Church Growth Movement

First, let us examine the history of the Church Growth movement. In order to understand it, we must go back to beginnings of the movement, to the life of Waskom Pickett.

The Input of Bishop Waskom Pickett

Bishop Waskom Pickett was short in stature and thin in build yet mighty in eloquence. Even in his retired years, when the churches in America really became acquainted with Bishop Pickett, he was a great inspiration and a dynamic preacher. For over forty years Bishop Pickett served the Methodist church as a missionary to India. He was vitally interested in the growth of the church and was personally responsible for hundreds of conversions.

The input of Bishop Waskom Pickett to the Church Growth movement started sometime after the turn of the century. A young man named Stanley, attending Asbury College, a small inter-denominational college with strong Wesleyan roots, became a room-mate of Waskom's. They shared a room in the Pickett's home in the college town of Wilmore, Kentucky. Stanley and Waskom were both "called" into the same mission field in India while they were roommates in those college days.

Both of these young missionaries went to India after being gradu-ated from college. Both became outstanding world leaders in mis-sion and evangelism. Stanley became known as the renowned evangelist and world traveler E. Stanley Jones. Waskom became a bishop of the Methodist church of India. They worked closely together and were each influenced by the other throughout their suc-cessful careers as missionaries. E. Stanley Jones is known for his fervent sermons toward winning the lost and Bishop Pickett for his abilities as an administrator and an assimilator of new converts into the life and work of the local church.

An investigation into the careers of these men will show how God prepared two young roomates for a large harvest over several decades in a foreign mission field. E. Stanley Jones and Bishop Waskom Pickett complemented one another in their efforts of winning and assimilating the lost. E. Stanley Jones was the evangelist and Bishop Waskom Pickett used his gifts of leadership to assimilate thousands into discipleship and commitment in the church.

Early in the 1930s, Waskom Pickett was a young missionary try-ing to be effective in his ministry. In the midst of his research and study he was perplexed. Why were some mission stations growing and winning the lost while others were not growing and were ineffec-tive at winning the lost? Through his research and study concerning this puzzling question, he wrote a book *Christian Mass Movements in India*. This book began to identify the reasons. When Dr. George Hunter asked the Bishop, a few years ago when interviewing him, why he did not continue to pursue his research in later years, Dr. Pickett replied that soon after his book was written he became a bishop. The resulting administrative pressures hindered his further research. The Bishop was, however, proud of his record as a bishop in relationship to the thousands he baptized and assimilated into the church. In 1972, I had a personal interview with the Bishop in Colum-bus, Ohio. At that time he assured me that, although E. Stanley Jones was an outstanding evangelist, it was his own efforts that assimilated thousands of new converts into the Methodist church in India.

E. Stanley Jones died in 1973. Bishop Waskom Pickett died in August, 1981. The imprint of the ministry of these two great leaders will be felt for generations to come.

The question is asked, "Who started the Church Growth movement?" The answer lies in Donald McGavran's summary of the movement's history.

> . . . *Many people have been involved in the discovery of church growth. While God has granted me a part in the process, I neither invented church growth nor am solely responsible for it. Indeed, I owe my interest in church growth to a great Methodist Bishop, Jarrell Waskom Pickett. In 1934, he kindled my concern that the church grow. I lit my candle at his fire. The Wesleyan Movement, which has been responsible for explosive church growth around the world for the last two centuries, was promoting church growth long before I was born. And the church has grown in many periods and cultures. Church growth has always been characteristic of healthy churches and basic to the power of the Christian movement. Today's church growth movement has, however, rediscovered church growth.* [1]

It must be noted here that the challenge for the church to grow has always been with us. The church has grown in some places in every century, yet the modern day movement was started by none other than an interested and curious Methodist missionary on a foreign mission field. Thus we can conclude that in Methodism, the modern church growth movement was founded.

The Influence of Donald McGavran and the Fuller School

Dr. C. Peter Wagner in his book, *Your Church Can Grow,* describes in his Introduction, "Where Did Church Growth Come From?", the history of the Church Growth movement.

> *Church growth as a movement entered North America in the fall of 1972. It took root in the mind and ministry of Donald McGavran while he was serving as third generation missionary to India over a period of thirty years. His first attempts at putting his ideas into writing date back to 1936.*

> *But the widespread diffusion of the movement began with his
> publication* The Bridges of God *(1955, Friendship Press) and* How
> Churches Grow *(1959, Friendship Press). These brought church
> growth, as it applied to world evangelization, to national and inter-
> national attention. The books were extensively reviewed in missionary
> journals on both sides of the Atlantic and around the world.*
>
> How Churches Grow *applies also to church growth in America.
> One of its chapters was reprinted as a booklet under the title* Do
> Churches Grow? *It sold some thousands of copies among Ameri-
> can church leaders, but failed to light any fires. The time was not
> yet ripe.* [2]

McGavran decided to move to Eugene, Oregon and found an
"Institute of Church Growth" at Northwest Christian College. Since
he had a background in the Christian church, the college was the
ideal place to start the institute. Classes in Church Growth began
there in 1961. His institute was intended for career missionaries on
furlough who could come to study and then return to the mission
field to share these new-found concepts with others.

By 1965 the institute had outgrown itself and it was reestablished
at Fuller Theological Seminary in Pasadena, California. From then
on it was called the School of World Mission and Institute of Church
Growth. [3]

The School at Fuller has grown greatly since its beginning and
today hundreds of graduates of the school are teaching others the
principles of Church Growth all around the world. However, the
concept of Church Growth did not catch on at first in the American
churches.

> *Since many American churches were not growing, church leaders
> and seminary professors had constructed an extensive defense partly
> theological, against church growth. This position glorified littleness
> and "quality" and maintained that growth in numbers is somewhat
> disreputable. One of McGavran's great contributions is his twenty-
> year assault on this non-biblical position.*
>
> *His magnum opus,* Understanding Church Growth *(Eerdmans)
> was published in 1970. It played a part in preparing America for
> church growth. It treated church growth on a global basis, vigor-
> ously exposed the fallacy of defense thinking, and started the*

19

universal principles which characterized it. He illustrated growth principles almost entirely from the expansion of churches overseas. It must be considered the Magna Carta of the church growth movement.[4]

In 1976, Dr. George Hunter, the Secretary of the Section on Evangelism of the Board of Discipleship of the United Methodist Church, took part of his associate staff and went to Fuller for intensive study into the principles of Church Growth. Upon returning from Pasadena to Nashville, Dr. Hunter and his staff began implementing the principles of Church Growth within evangelism strategies for his denomination. Other denominational leaders simultaneously began catching the Church Growth fever. The Episcopal Church, the Lutheran bodies, and other denominations began sending their leaders to Fuller. Dr. Hunter has since taught many church growth seminars in churches, districts and conferences. He has written *The Contagious Congregation* and, with Dr. McGavran, has co-authored *Church Growth Strategies That Work*. Both books are recognized by church growth leaders as significant treatments of the subject. Dr. Hunter is now the Dean of the E. Stanley Jones School of Mission and Evangelism at Asbury Seminary.

For a few summers after Dr. Hunter studied at Fuller, he taught a basic Church Growth I seminar to Master of Arts in Evangelism students at Scarritt College in Nashville, Tennessee. The author was one of those students taking Church Growth I in Nashville in the summer of 1977.

Thus the history of the Church Growth movement included both the input of Bishop Waskom Pickett and the influence of Donald McGavran and the Fuller School. Church Growth principles, which now appeal to many in all denominations, have their historical foundations in the life and input of Pickett and McGavran.

The History of the Wesleyan Movement

For a complete understanding of the modern Church Growth Movement, we must see its relationship to the history of the Wesleyan Movement. The Wesleyan Movement was founded in a spirit of church planting and growth. The founding father of the Wesleyan Movement was committed to winning the lost and incorporating those lost who became found into societies of believers. These societies later became churches and the ministry of John Wesley was multiplied.

> *After thirty years, in 1768, Methodism had forty circuits and 27,341 members. Ten years later the numbers had grown to sixty circuits and 40,089 members; in another decade, ninety-nine circuits and 66,375 members. By 1789, several years after Wesley's death, the totals had jumped to one hundred forty circuits with 101,712 members. This is the stuff that church growth charts are made of.[5]*

John Wesley's zeal and unusual talents were the keys to this great growth over a few short years. He was applying the principles of Church Growth. He may have been unaware of that. It was his expectation, however, that churches would, by that very nature, grow.

> *Wesley was not a systematic theologian as, for example, was Calvin. In his busy life he rarely pursued his study of doctrine long enough to work all the subtle details into adequate systematic form. In this respect he is not unlike Luther.[6]*

His sermons are great sources of his systematic doctrine which he preached to plain folk. He preached these sermons everywhere, in Church of England parish churches, in factories, in the coal mines, on the street corners, and in the parks. He would preach to a few and he often preached to thousands.

John Wesley never relinquished his membership or ordination in the Church of England. However, the new methodical group movement he instituted from his position as an Anglican priest became a denomination after his death. He had considered severing his societies from the mother church during his years of leadership but ". . . the break did not become official until after his death."[7] His interest was in helping people become vital believers so he gave little attention to developing a new denomination. He worked hard at developing these societies into strong person-centered groups. In his own words Wesley told, at the end of his ministerial career, how these societies were formed:

> *In the latter end of the year 1739, eight or ten persons came to me in London, who appeared to be deeply convinced of sin, and earnestly groaning for redemption. They desired (as did two or three more the next day) that I would spend some time with them in prayer,*

and advise them how to flee from the wrath to come; which they saw continually hanging over their heads. That we might have more time for this great work, I appointed a day when they might all come together, which from thenceforward they did every week, namely, on Thursday, in the evening. To these, and as many more as desired to join them, (for their number increased daily) I gave those advices, from time to time, which I judged most needful for them; and we always concluded our meeting with prayer suited to their several necessities. [8]

Wesley wrote that these Thursday evening meetings developed into the United Society. First, in London, they then spread to other communities. He called these societies a company of men seeking godliness, praying together, exhorting one another from the Word and watching over one another in love. These fervent actions were designed to enable each to help the other work out his or her individual salvation. [9]

Wesley described how these small groups began:

That it may the more easily be discerned, whether they are indeed working out their own salvation, each society is divided into smaller companies called classes, *according to their respective places of abode. There are about twelve persons in every class; one of whom is styled the* Leader. [10]

Not only was it the leader's business to see each person in his "class" once a week, to determine the state of his soul; he was also to meet with the minister and the stewards of the society once a week. The meeting with the minister and stewards was to inform the minister of those who were sick and those who were "walking disorderly." The meeting with the stewards was to review the collections from the meetings. [11]

These United Societies and the smaller classes were the backbone of the growth which results from those humble beginnings. Within these roots the principles of Church Growth were formulated and implemented in the methodologies of this great leader and founder of Methodism.

Concerned about commitment among his followers, Wesley intended the class meetings to prompt that desired commitment. He tried to be an example to his followers by practicing Christian perfection in his daily life. In his *Journal* Wesley recorded his thought following a letter he had written to the editor of *Lloyd's Evening Post* on March 5, 1767. The letter was a defense against editors of Christian magazines who had been attacking him and his followers because of his call to perfection. He defended himself and the new movement by providing background into his own life regarding the emphasis upon Christian perfection. He originally had published a pamphlet entitled "The Character of a Methodist," which stressed the importance of his followers living in perfection. He felt the message in his pamphlet had obviously been misunderstood by those outside the Methodist movement. His greatest concern, however, was that his critics were making light of his own Christian perfection:

> *Sir, have me excused. This is not "according to Mr. Wesley." I have told all the world I am not perfect; and yet you allow me to be a Methodist. I tell you flatly, I have not attained the character I draw. Will you pin it upon me in spite of my teeth?"*
>
> *"But Mr. Wesley says, the other Methodists have." I say no such thing. What I say, after having given a scriptural account of a perfect Christian, is this: "By these marks the Methodists desire to be distinguished from other men; by these we labor to distinguish ourselves." And do not you yourself desire and labor after the same very thing?*[12]

He concluded his "letter to the editor" by affirming that Methodists must trust in the mercy of God and not their own righteousness. The emphasis upon Christian perfection is to seek to find the kind of life which will lead the believer closer to God and his mercy.

The striving for Christian perfection was the holy lifestyle which Wesley expected of each faithful convert. Anyone not exemplifying that lifestyle was politely asked to disbar himself or herself from the fellowship. Anything less than this kind of holy commitment was not enough. The early circuit riders were expected to live in the same holy lifestyle. Their preaching was to be fulfillment of their own personal commitment. Wesley was more than vigorous in his defense of the movement and verbally combative for his defense when anyone misunderstood or misinterpreted its goals.

Wesley's statement on Christian perfection concluded with these words:

Why should devout men be afraid of devoting all their soul, body, and substance to God? Why should those who love Christ count it a damnable error to think we may have all the mind that was in Him? We allow, we contend, that we are justified freely through the righteousness and the blood of Christ. And why are you so hot against us, because we expect likewise to be sanctified wholly through His Spirit? We look for no favour either from the open servants of sin, or from those who have only the form of religion.[13]

Thus the founder of the Wesleyan Movement sought committed followers. He wanted nothing less than the best from his followers and he expected the same from himself. For Wesley, discipleship was the name of the game and striving for perfection was the theological base for finding that kind of life.

In his *Journal* Wesley described the accomplishments of his ministry after some fifty years. The growth and outreach of the cause may possibly be unmatchable.

Thursday, March 24 (Worcester). I was now considering how strangely the grain of mustard seed, planted about fifty years ago, has grown up. It has spread through all Great Britain and Ireland; the Isle of Wight, and the Isle of Man; then to America, from the Leeward Islands through the whole continent into Canada and Newfoundland. And the societies, in all these parts, walk by one rule, knowing religion is holy tempers; striving to worship God, not in form only, but likewise in spirit and in truth.[14]

The church grew those first fifty years because of the proper planting of biblical seeds for growth. Wesley expected discipleship and commitment and the results were a great new church spreading across the seas and reaching the masses and the classes in the new world.

Even in his last year Wesley was still about his Father's business:

Sunday, 24, — I explained, to a numerous congregation in Spitalfields Church, "the whole armor of God." St. Paul's, Shadwell, was still more crowded in the afternoon while I enforced that important truth, "One thing is needful"; and I hope many, even then, resolved to choose the better part.[15]

From these beginnings, the history of the Wesleyan movement

was one of a transcontinental church that was to gain many followers and much power in the next two centuries. The growth of this small group, which became an instrument for God, manifested itself most profoundly in the North American continent in the following two hundred years.

Church in America

At the beginning of the formation of the United States of America there was a great need for the presentation of the gospel of Jesus Christ. A new nation was forming and the inspiration of the gospel was being felt — from simple farm folk to respected government leaders. The leadership of John Wesley carried over to the new nation through his many circuit riders. They came to this country and began crossing and crisscrossing it with a revivalistic passion to save the lost.

In the middle of the eighteenth century when young evangelists who had shared John Wesley's heart-warming experience appeared in New York and Maryland and began to form classes and circuits of the people called Methodists, America presented a most complicated religious pattern.[16]

Nine of the thirteen colonies had established churches with no one denomination holding the majority of the people of the colonies. In the fall of 1768 Wesley was advised of the need to send pastors and evangelists to the American continent.

The following August, 1769, at the Conference at Leeds, John Wesley stated from the chair, "We have a pressing call from our brethren of New York (who have built a preaching house) to come over and help them." He then asked, "Who is willing to go?" and then and there two preachers offered themselves for this service — Richard Boardman and Joseph Pilmoor.[17]

The next month those missionaries set sail from Bristol and arrived a few miles below Philadelphia on October 24th.

A little group of Methodists were awaiting them. having been informed of their coming by letter from Doctor Wrangel. Immediately the English preachers began their work, Pilmoor preaching from the steps of the Old State House, now known as Independence Hall, on Chestnut Street.[18]

This was the beginning of the Methodist church in America. Little was Wesley to know how great a church in the new world he was building.

> *In the year 1770 the name "America" made its first appearance in the list of Wesley's Conference appointments, with the names of four American preachers — Joseph Pilmoor, Richard Broadman, Robert Williams, and John King. The next year (1771) the English Minutes record three hundred and sixteen members in the American societies, while during the year appeals continued to reach Wesley especially from Captain Webb, Broadman, and Pilmoor, asking that more preachers be sent to America.* [19]

The church was small in its beginnings but grew rapidly, as the increases indicate. The vast urban and suburban churches which dot the landscape of North America today were begun in tiny settlements during those early years. The circuit riders went from village to village and rural area to rural area evangelizing the settlers. These traveling evangelists started societies in each community where they had a nucleus of believers. The societies later blossomed into churches and church buildings were the results of regular gathering of the new believers. The early church grew from the three hundred and sixteen members recorded in 1771 to (combining Evangelical United Brethren and Methodist) just over eleven million members of 1965. The 1965 total was the highest total recorded in the church's history.

Thus in a little over two hundred years a great church was developed and nurtured. There were two evident reasons why the United Methodist church grew into what it is today. One was the strong leadership of the circuit riders. These faithful men of God were dynamic and able as they led individuals and groups to Christ. In terms of today's program for ministry preparation, they were lay preachers; few of them had any formal schooling.

The other reason the United Methodist Church grew into what it is today is that there was great commitment on the part of the laity. These lay leaders were willing to risk their lives and their reputations in order to win the lost. The clergy and the laity together were able to reach the lost. From its small beginnings with the early settlers, the church has grown into one of the largest denominations in America.

Church Growth Principles in
Small Town and Rural Churches

If the small town and rural churches of today are to grow, they must embrace the principles of Church Growth. Past successes are always linked to strong leadership by clergy and laity. C. Peter Wagner lists seven vital signs for Church Growth today. The first two on his list are the same ingredients which made the church grow:

> *One, a pastor who is a possibility thinker and whose dynamic leadership has been used to catalyze the entire church into action for growth. Second, a well-mobilized laity which has discovered, has developed and is using all the spiritual gifts for growth.* [20]

Church history is filled with examples of strong growth led by a strong clergy and laity.

The powerful leadership of the early American preachers was a great influence for good on the church's growth. From all accounts we read about these leaders, we find they were people who believed in a specific "calling" by God to bring individuals to Christ. While living under spartan existence, they made much personal sacrifice in order to bring their calling to fruition. Many were exposed to the elements. Failing health due to excessive work was their common job hazard. Thus many of them died after only a few short years of ministry.

Not only did these early American preachers have to contend with their own human frailty; the immoral character of the early settlements was almost too much for these early traveling evangelists to endure. In reference to early Methodist preachers, Dr. William Sweet says, "As Methodism extended into the expanding frontiers in every direction, the preachers were soon brought face to face with the distressing moral conditions common to the new and rude communities." [21] It was common to find in a community lawlessness, rowdyism, and fighting, brought on by the age-old problem with alcoholic beverages. For those who were total abstainers the road was rather rough. The famous circuit rider Peter Cartwright reported,

> *. . . That if a man would not have liquor in his family, his harvest, his houseraisings, log-rollings, and weddings, he would be "considered parsimonious and unsociable," and even professing Christians would not help a man at his log-rollings and in his harvest if he did not furnish liquor and treat the company.* [22]

Because of these social standards, the preachers had much difficulty bringing the gospel to these communities. Yet the tireless efforts of many of them brought church growth as a reward.

These effective preachers were mostly uneducated. They were found lacking in the kind of extensive training experienced by today's minister. Because of their lack of formal education, they stressed the need for it among their converts. Thus, because they stressed the need for education, today most of the great institutions of higher learning found their roots in the efforts of these early American preachers.

Moreover, the early American preachers planted the seeds of learning in their churches. Through long hours of personal labor in the Scriptures, they inspired their followers to spend time in study. The early church began to grow in wisdom as well as stature. Since those early days the church has stressed the importance of formal education. Thus today in most denominations one cannot be fully ordained a minister without four years of college and three years of post-graduate school in an approved seminary.

Through this process of more and more emphasis on education, the freshness and innocence of the early preachers has been lost. Many young men and women become excited about their calling into ministry, only to seemingly have that excitement dampened by the seven years of higher education. Their early zeal is lost in the midst of scholarly requirements. The complaint of many churches who receive these men and women after seminary is that they have so much "head knowledge" that they have lost the personal heart-felt conviction they also need.

If success is to be realized in town and rural churches, we must combine the "heart warming" experience of the Wesleyan revival of the past with a proper stress upon the intellect which our seminaries have to offer us today. From early on pastors sought growth. He came to a town and saw the possibilities for growth in the rowdy and unreligious frontier. His dynamic leadership tranformed those communities into righteous and religious fortresses of faith. The church he was nurturing recognized his leadership and accepted his abilities.

If we, as clergy and laity, can combine "heart experience" with "head experience," we can once again raise up a vital growing small town and rural church. The young clergy of today are capable of catalyzing the church into great growth in the years ahead. By reflecting upon the example of our forefathers of the frontier, who led the church into marvelous growth, we can gain a base to accomplish the same growth today. This dynamic principle of pastoral leadership which worked so effectively in our heritage is the first vital sign suggested by C. Peter Wagner. Since this principle of pastoral leadership worked for the early American churches, before the modern Church Growth movement began, and is working for the Church Growth movement today, it can and will work for us in the small town and rural churches now and in the future.

The second vital sign on C. Peter Wagner's list is *the well-mobilized laity*. The laity is often the great untapped reservoir of ability which many a church overlooks. A quick look again into past history reveals that the early American church's laity was alive and well. The early American preachers visited the local societies, Sunday church schools and churches once a month at the most. Yet, they left in charge capable laypeople who led those societies, Sunday church schools, and churches in between pastoral visits. When a preacher came to the church, he found it usually capably led by these lay leaders who had discovered and were actively using their spiritual gifts to bring new life to the society. Many times the circuit rider would find several new converts activated since his last visit.

The new interest in mobilizing the laity today among our denominational folk is a good sign. This lay witness movement is a healthy fresh breeze, mobilizing laity to do what they can do for the church. The movement is raising scores of lay persons from all sections of the country who are ready, willing and able to use their gifts to evangelize the church. Many of the churches have succeeded to commissioning the laity to go out and win the lost. These new stirrings are in our roots. The early church of the later 1700s was able effectively to evangelize through the laity. Now the lay witness movement is mobilizing the laity today. As we have evangelized through our laity in the past, we are beginning to do so again today.

The Church Growth pastor and a gifted laity, then, are part of the history of our churches. We are seeing them successful again today. It does not matter precisely how laity and clergy are energized, so long as an impetus for growth is passed along, denominations stop declining and true growth is stimulated. Since a solid tradition of both Church Growth pastor and gifted laity are already in our heritage, we cannot help but wish to strengthen interest in their reemergence today.

From my own studies, research and application of Church Growth principles over the past ten years, I can affirm that C. Peter Wagner's first two vital signs are indeed the main ingredients which make all other principles work. If a church is to grow, it needs a pastor who is dynamically leading the church into growth and a laity with knowledge of and eagerness to implement their spiritual gifts. These two vital signs are essential for the workings of all other Church Growth principles.

The small town and rural congregations, which make up seventy-five percent of our churches today can grow again. They can grow again by applying the principles of Church Growth. These principles were operative in the early days and they are practical today.

Questions for Discussion of Chapter 1

1. Who was the originator of the modern day Church Growth movement?

2. In your own words explain the two Church Growth principles listed in this chapter.

3. How can these two principles be effective today in your church?

4. In your own words, give reasons why churches stop growing.

5. Give your reasons as to how the small town or rural church can grow.

Footnotes

[1]Hunter and McGavran, *Church Growth Strategies That Work,* p. 14.

[2]C. Peter Wagner, *Your Church Can Grow* (Glendale: G/L Regal Books, A Division of G/L Publications, 1976), p. 11.

[3]Wagner, *Your Church Can Grow,* p. 12-13.

[4]Wagner, *Your Church Can Grow,* p. 14.

[5]Howard Snyder, *The Radical Wesley* (Downers Grove: Inter-Varsity Press, 1980), p. 54.

[6]Robert W. Burtner and Robert E. Chiles, *A Compend of Wesley's Theology* (New York: Abingdon Press, 1954), p. 7.

[7]*Ibid.,* p. 253.

[8]*Ibid.,* p. 257-258.

[9]*Ibid.,* p. 258.

[10]*Ibid.,* p. 258.

[11]*Ibid.,* p. 258.

[12]*The Journal of John Wesley,* ed. by Percy Livingstone Parker (Chicago: Moody Press, n.d.), p. 292.

[13]John Wesley, *A Plain Account of Christian Perfection* (London: The Epworth Press, n.d.) pp. 110-111.

[14]*The Journal of John Wesley,* p. 395.

[15]*Ibid.,* p. 415.

[16]William Warren Sweet, *Methodism in American History* (Nashville: Abingdon Press, 1953), p. 9.

[17]*Ibid.,* p. 47-48.

[18]*Ibid.,* p. 48.

[19]*Ibid.,* p. 63.

[20]C. Peter Wagner, *Your Church Can Grow* (Glendale: Regal Books, 1976), p. 159.

[21]Sweet, p. 169.

[22]Sweet, p. 170.

Chapter 2

A Case Study: United Methodist Distinctives as Viewed from the Perspective of the Church at Ephesus

Mainline denominations are in a period of decline today. Something drastic must be done to turn this *de*cline into an *in*cline. We need to reverse the down-and-out mindset. We need now to experience an upward renewal. While this chapter could be written from the perspective of any mainline group, I wish to focus on my own denomination, the United Methodist Church, in these next pages. Since the United Methodist Church is the largest of the mainline denominations, and has suffered serious recent decline, let us look at it in the context of the Church at Ephesus and the challenge this poses for its renewal.

The United Methodist church has two important theological distinctives which are of primary importance for Church Growth. These are: (a) the filling of the Holy Spirit, or the baptism of love; and (b) the divine imperative to evangelize. Historically, the church has focused on these two distinctives. In recent years their emphasis has become secondary instead of primary. When Dr. George Hunter III, now the Dean of the E. Stanley Jones School at Asbury Seminary, was a professor of Evangelism at Perkins School of Theology in 1974, he became interested in the Church Growth movement. He later audited the Church Growth courses at Fuller Seminary offered by Dr. Donald McGavran and Dr. C. Peter Wagner. He came home recommitted to the task of kindling a renewal of these two distinctives in the church.

I first heard Dr. Hunter speak during course work in 1977, while I was completing a Master of Arts in Evangelism at Scarritt College in Nashville, Tennessee. Dr. Hunter introduced to me the principles of Church Growth. Committed to seeing the church recapture the distinctives of love and evangelism, he introduced the profound idea that the first love of the church ought to be evangelism. Love and evangelism go hand in hand. The Wesleyan emphasis upon the Holy Spirit's work among believers is ultimately brought to fruition when new converts are conceived, birthed, nurtured and matured.

Dr. Hunter warned that the United Methodist Church was like the church at Ephesus (see in Revelation, Chaper Two), a church which had lost its first love.

Following this introduction to Church Growth by Dr. Hunter, I began to piece together the uniqueness of the Wesleyan principle of love and the need to re-emphasize evangelism in the Wesleyan spirit. These distinctives, interwoven into the principles of Church Growth, can be a powerful impetus for the United Methodist Church to re-establish itself as a vital, growing denomination. They can also be applied to any denomination or local church.

Let us now see how these distinctives, viewed in the context of the church at Ephesus, can impact large segments of our population in general and small town and rural church settings in particular.

The Church at Ephesus "Lost its First Love"
(Revelation 2)

The message the angel gave the church at Ephesus in Revelation, Chapter Two, included the statement that the church had "lost its first love." This same diagnosis needs to be made for the United Methodist Church today and for the mainline churches as a whole. I first heard this statement from Dr. George Hunter that same summer in 1977, as did more than sixty other United Methodist ministers. This group of ministers was not the first to hear Dr. Hunter say it, however. He had previously made the same statement in messages to the Council of Bishops, several Annual Conferences, and to whomever else would listen to his presentation. Dr. Hunter was the head of the Section of Evangelism of the United Methodist Church, the denomination which had been losing membership at an alarming rate since peaking at just over eleven million members in 1965. The same loss of membership has been experienced by mainline denominations.

Having taken Dr. Hunter's message to the church as a personal challenge, I began studying the Second chapter of Revelation and reflecting upon its application to our denomination and to the mainline churches. I concluded that he was indeed correct. I found the local church — the one I was then serving — to be a church that had "lost its first love". Furthermore, the fifty churches with which I worked when leading Church Growth Seminars had the same problem.

Permit me to compare both the strengths and the weaknesses of the church at Ephesus with those of the United Methodist Church (or fill in your own denominational name). Let me begin with the strengths. There are four:

a. The church had pride.
b. The church was proper.
c. The church had perseverance.
d. The church was pure.

In Revelation 2:2 *pride* is described as a strength. The Ephesians were a hardworking church, as are the denominations today. American Christianity has some of the most attractive places of worship humankind could ever erect. The sanctuaries and educational units exhibit to their respective communities that Christians are hardworking people. The Protestant work ethic is demonstrated in our lives as individuals and also is seen in our places of worship. It is a proper pride.

The second strength of the church at Ephesus was this: the church was *proper*. The angel said "I know your deeds." (Revelation 2:2) The church at Ephesus was a church that did things right — for themselves and for others. So do American mainline denominations. They are known for their accomplishments, for deeds well done. For its part, the United Methodist Church has, from the beginning, helped the underprivileged and the needy. It has many hospitals and homes for the aged all over the country.

The church at Ephesus had a third strength: perseverance. "You have persevered and have endured hardships for my name, and have not grown weary." (Revelation 2:3) The same can be said of the American mainline. For over two hundred years the United Methodist Church has persevered and endured. It is a strong church today because it has not grown weary. So, too, with Episcopalians, Presbyterians, Lutherans.

The Ephesus church was a pure church. "I know that you cannot tolerate wicked men, that you have tested those who claim to be apostles but are not, and have found them false." (Revelation 2:2b) As in other denominations, purity is a strength of the United Methodist Church. From the local Pastor-Parish Committee to the District Board of Ordained Ministry to the Conference Board of Ordained Ministry, the process towards ordination for clergy is long and laborious. Because of this system, the United Methodist Church may remove any clergy candidates who are not acceptable. Young ministers-to-be might complain about the study and interviewing involved within the system; yet it produces the proper results. The church at Ephesus (Revelation 2:6b) "hated the practices in the Nicolaitans, which I also hate." The Nicolaitans were those who practiced sexual immorality. Any Christian denomination today would stand against sexual immorality. Whenever a United Methodist minister is involved in immoral conduct, the Pastor-Parish Committee meets to recommend his/her removal. There are then, clear parallels between the strengths of the church at Ephesus and the American church today.

However, the *weakness* of church at Ephesus also surfaces in our generation. "Yet I hold this against you: You have forsaken your first love." (Revelation 2:4) "Remember the height from which you have fallen! Repent, and do the things you did at first." (Revelation 2:5) What does the angel mean when he says the Ephesians have forsaken their first love? The meaning is clear: they have stopped evangelizing. The first generation Ephesian Christians were evangelistic. Their new-found love for Christ, following their conversions, excited them to share that treasure with others. Their infectious witness brought others to Christ and the church multiplied. However, a few years later, their children who grew up in their parents' church and accepted their parents' religion were not as excited about sharing the faith.

The conversion of the children and later the children's children is called "biological growth" in Church Growth terminology. The conversion of the individual from the world is called "conversion growth." The third possible means of growth is called "tranfer growth." This occurs when someone transfers from one congregation to another. Therefore, by the time John received his revelation, the church at Ephesus was a few family-generations old, and the only new converts in their local body were their children and children's children and those moving into their communities from other churches who were recommended to their body by Paul or Silas or one of the other missionaries. They were by then a proud, proper, persevering and pure church — but *their only growth was inward, or biological.* The angel warned them to return to the winning of the lost, as they had done at first when they were growing and multiplying as a first-generation church.

The United Methodist Church was a great church in the late 1700s. Conversion growth was spectacular. The early circuit riders were about the business of winning the lost. As our country grew rapidly, with westward expansion, with settlers on the move in the 1800s, the young Methodist denomination continued to grow by conversion growth because, as new communities were developed so were new churches started, and the church grew and prospered. With the rapid influx of immigrants in the early 1900s and the resulting population explosion, the denomination continued to grow because new churches were started and new groups of people gathered. Throughout this whole period the practice of biological growth and transfer growth was strong.

But sometime around the middle of this century the church ceased to gain more than it lost. During the year 1965, membership statistics show that the membership of the United Methodist Church, which included the Evangelical United Brethren Church, peaked at 11.1 million members.[1] *Since that year membership has declined every single year.* In 1968, at the time of the merger, the two denominations had a membership of just under 11 million members. By 1975 the membership had dropped to under 10 million.[2] The membership figures from the United Methodist Church were over 9.6 million in 1980 (*The Interpreter,* March-April, 1982, page 30). Since then it has declined even more, to less than 9.5 million. All the mainline denominations show similar declines. The obvious reason for the decline has been failure to win new converts.

The church at Ephesus "lost its first love." The warning from the angel is severe. "If you do not repent, I will come to you and remove your lampstand from its place." (Revelation 2:5b) In Revelation 1:12 and 13 the golden lampstands representing each of the seven churches are mentioned. In the midst of the lampstands "was someone like a son of man." (Revelation 1:13) The lampstands suggest the prominence of the Spirit of Christ in the church. The warning, then, was that the Holy Spirit, as the empowerment of the church at Ephesus, would be removed from prominence if the Ephesians did not repent. (Revelation 2:5) Evangelism without the power of the Holy Spirit is useless. The angel is promising the removal of the Holy Spirit from the church unless the church once again uses the Spirit of the Evangel to win the lost and enable conversion growth. The results would be disastrous to a church that had many strengths.

Since the United Methodist Church and all the other mainline denominations are parallel the church at Ephesus, they too can suffer the same disastrous results. All our mainline churches are based on a holy faith. The power of the Holy Spirit is held sacred at the center of each denomination's traditions, but their failure to *use* the Holy Spirit's empowerment to win the lost and return to the basics in conversion growth invites the same serious warning. Our churches must repent and once again allow the Holy Spirit to work among us. The mainline churches must look to the Scriptures and God's Spirit for leadership. The United Methodist Church must allow the Spirit to work through it as the evangel, to bring conversion to the lost. The United Methodist Church has the distinctives of love and evangelism as its roots. It must bring salvation to the lost again as its message, and those who are thus converted will be the fruit of that effort. The church then — and only then — will have repented. The lost will have been found and the warning to the church at Ephesus some 2,000 years ago will have been heeded today. American Christianity needs to return to its first love, just as the church at Ephesus was challenged to return to its first love.

The Uniqueness of the Wesleyan Principle of Love

The Wesleyan principle of love is unique. The Wesleyan movement has given humanity this unique principle. The Wesleyan revival of eighteenth century England is an example of that principle of love applied. The church at Ephesus and the United Methodist Church are alike in their need to return to their first love. The United Methodist Church needs to return to its principle of love which was dramatized by its evangelistic zeal during the eighteenth century revival.

Poverty, vice, drunkenness, injustice, and corruption were everywhere. The churches were empty and the jails full. In 1750 over eleven million gallons of gin were consumed in England, much of it in

38

circumstances similar to those portrayed by William Hogarth in "Gin Lane" and other paintings. The Church of England had over eleven thousand livings in the kingdom — positions for clergymen paid from state revenues — of which six thousand were occupied by men who did not deign to go near the parishes they were paid to serve, but farmed them out to poorly paid curates and themselves went to live luxuriously in London or on the Continent.[3]

Crime was on the rampage. Prisoners received inhuman treatment. The treatment of orphans and other children of paupers was equally inhuman. The country was ripe for revival and the message of the great John Wesley powerfully challenged England's culture and way of life. Some of the wrongdoers of English society were completely transformed in a beautiful way and became champions themselves of the underprivileged and downcast.

Under this diligent tutelage, the followers of the Wesleys became noted for their honesty, thrift, industry, and zeal. Many who had been drunkards and petty thieves became sober and hardworking pillers of their class meetings.[4]

The emphasis of the changed heart was at the center of all Wesley's preaching. He was not interested in bringing individuals and groups of people to salvation and salvation alone in order to see their names recorded in heaven. Wesley was interested in bringing individuals and groups of people into a completely different lifestyle, one in which the power of love permeated their every act, word or deed.

On January 1, 1733, Wesley preached before Oxford University in St. Mary's Church on the theme of the circumcision of the heart. In that sermon he said,

It is that habitual disposition of soul, which directly implied the being cleansed from sin; from all filthiness both of flesh and spirit; and, by consequence, the being endued with those virtues which were in Christ Jesus; the being so "renewed in the image of our mind," as to be "perfect as our Father in heaven is perfect."[5]

Wesley clarified his unique principle of love in that same sermon to the Oxford University community.

*"Love is the fulfilling of the law, the end of the commandment."
It is not only the first and great command, but all the command-
ments in one: "Whatsoever things are just, whatsoever things are
pure, if there be any virtue, if there be any praise," they are all com-
prised in this one word, Love. In this is perfection, and glory, and
happiness.* [6]

Wesley believed this divine experience called love was the royal law
of heaven and earth. Believers are to love God with everything they
have and to demonstrate that love to others. The greatest demon-
stration of that love for others is to win them to him. The fruit of
the love the believer has in Christ is fulfilled in bringing those outside Christ into his fellowship and glory. Wesley said, concerning
this resulting fruit, "One thing shall ye desire for its own sake: the
fruition of Him who is all in all." [7]

Wesley concluded his remarks by bringing to light the ultimate
of the Christian experience, the circumcision of the heart. God wants
those who follow him to accept the fullness of his law, perfect law.
This perfect law results in a heart changed by the act of circumcision. From this act of circumcision the heart is transformed into love.
Wesley said of this experience, "Let your soul be filled with so entire a love to [Christ], that you may love nothing but for his sake.
Have a pure intention of heart, a steadfast regard to his glory in
all your actions." [8] Then ultimately the believer has the mind of
Christ. To have the mind of Christ is to his will and his pleasure.

At this point the Wesleyan concept of circumcision of the heart
"coincides with the call to the Ephesians to return to your first love."
The first love of the Christian is a subservience to the love of God
in Christ. The will of Christ was to evangelize the lost. Therefore,
the mind of Christ was to evangelize the lost. Therefore, the mind
of Christ was centered on evangelism and the desire of those being
circumcised with his Spirit is for evangelizing the lost. The great love
Christ had for the lost was demonstrated in his giving himself as
a sacrifice for those lost. The call to the church at Ephesus was to
return to that kind of experience with Christ, and to bear such fruit.
The evangelization of the lost is the calling of the church. When the
believers lost that zeal for the lost, the church becomes ineffective.

Change of heart for the sake of evangelism was at the center
of Wesley's personal life and preaching. Though Wesley spoke
these words early in his ministry, he continued to believe them

wholeheartedly throughout the rest of his ministry. He was interested in bringing people into the kind of relationship with God which would completely change their lives, so that they, in turn, would influence the changing of those people with whom they associated.

The results of this bold preaching upon England in the eighteenth century is history. The results upon early America by Wesley's followers is also history. However, history has yet to record the results concerning the impact of the Wesleyan principle of love for the remaining years of this century. The opportunity to record them as a positive witness is in the hands of the present United Methodist Church and mainline Christianity in general. All of our churches must accept the challenge of that message to the church at Ephesus and return to our first love. We must once again become diligent about living the Christian life in the true holiness lifestyle. Then history will record that principle of love had changed individuals and culture in America during the latter part of this century.

This principle of love can prove fruitful in the life of the rural and small town church. The kind of Christian community which Wesley espoused can develop in our rural areas of America as we challenge ourselves to be faithful to total commitment and evangelism to Christ.

A chicken and a pig were walking down a country road one hot August evening. They came upon a country church and immediately noticed a large number of cars parked around it. The pig said to the chicken, "Look, there must be a revival going on in there. Let us go in and see. I have not been to a revival in years." The chicken agreed and together they went into the church. After they arrived inside, they could not see anyone in the sanctuary. Hearing noises in the social hall, they entered only to find the whole congregation involved in planning a church supper. The people were so busy and excited about their planning, they didn't notice the entrance of the chicken and the pig. The two of them sat in the corner and listened. One group was planning the table decorations. Another group was the hospitality committee. Another group was working on tickets and finances. Still another group was planning the menu. From this group the chicken and pig found out it was a ham and eggs dinner. By then the chicken was totally caught up in the excitement. She leaned over to the pig and said, "Come on, let us join in and offer our services for the dinner."

The pig answered quickly, "Oh, no. For you it would be a

one-time contribution. But for me it would be total commitment.''

The uniqueness of the Wesleyan principle of love is tied up in the reality of what the pig would have to offer — total commitment. Wesley preached for total commitment. The totality of the Wesleyan commitment made it distinctive from any other commitment. It was a total commitment to the power of God through the Holy Spirit. The essence of the commitment was love. That love is best manifested in the believers giving themselves to others in love. The results would mean bringing those others from outside of Christ into fellowship with Him.

Total commitment means being used of God for his glory. His glory is manifested when others are being won to him. This result is first-love commitment.

The Rediscovery of Evangelism in the Wesleyan Spirit

If the United Methodist Church and other mainline denominations are to return to the kind of evangelism with which they began, they will need to rediscover the meaning of the gospel. In order to recapture the United Methodist Church's understanding of evangelism in the Wesleyan spirit, we must accept the necessity for the church to return to its ''first love'' and accept the requirement to embrace the implications of the gospel. Small town and rural churches must see this necessity and return to their first love.

The Necessity of the Church to Return to Its ''First Love''

The small town and rural church must understand that it is essential to return to its first love, the love of winning the lost. The history of the church reminds us that reaching the lost is the essence of the gospel, and that the church most effectively accomplished that kind of evangelism in its beginnings.

Small town and rural churches can lead the way to first-love evangelism. They represent seventy-five percent of the total churches of all mainline denominations. The very culture which they have nurtured has historically been — and still is — conducive to evangelism of the Wesleyan type.

The Need to Understand the Implications of the Gospel

The gospel message is predicated with the truth that "all have sinned," (Romans 3:23, KJV); that "there is none righteous," (Romans 3:10, KJV); and that "all we like sheep have gone astray." (Isaiah 53:6, KJV) The gospel message calls for repentance. The sinner must repent or suffer the consequences: eternal death. Without confession of sin the unrepentant is doomed for eternal death without God. By confessing his or her sin a person is justified by Christ to live forever with God both here and in heaven. These scriptural truths and their theological implications must be understood and accepted in order truly to re-emphasize evangelism in the Wesleyan Spirit.

Moreover, without Christ, the unrepentant is doomed forever. Those involved with evangelism in the Wesleyan Spirit need to be filled with a loving urgency to bring the unrepentant to repentance in Christ. The time is now, today, before it is too late.

The Spirit of Wesleyan Evangelism Can
Reach Large Segments of Our Population

The church can repent of its failure to be about its commitment to winning the lost. The church can re-emphasize evangelism in the Wesleyan spirit. It *can be done if the church and its leaders are willing.* With willing leaders we will have found the way for the spirit of Wesleyan evangelism to reach large segments of our population. The way to accomplish this monumental task is by returning to first-love evangelism. If we love the Lord with our whole lives, as we are called to in the first great commandment, and if we love our neighbor as ourselves, in response to the second great commandment, then we must be willing and ready to win these neighbors to him, so that they too will know him as do we. This is truly a challenging task, but the challenge can be met, and large segments of our population can be reached.

Therefore, large segments of our population can be reached for Christ with planned and strategized evangelism which is filled with Wesley's teachings. Those who evangelize must strive for perfection. (In some denominations the preferred term is "sanctification.") The Wesleyan teachings on Christian perfection — holiness, godly living, zeal for God's Kingdom — must be reinstituted into the teachings and practices of the denominational and independent churches and their leaders. The biblical standard of perfection (or sanctification) must again be the standard of any renewal movement of today. When Wesley was questioned on how to avoid setting the standard for Christian behavior "too high" or "too low," he answered:

> By keeping the Bible, and setting it just as high as the Scripture does. It is not higher and nothing lower than this — the pure love of God and man, the loving God with all our heart and soul, and our neighbor as ourselves. It is love governing the heart and life, running through all our tempers, words, and actions.[9]

We need to set our standards as high as our early fathers did in the beginnings of our churches. This strategy is needed to win large segments of our society to Christ. It is a simply defined yet difficult-to-live challenge. The small town and rural churches have traditionally kept the emphasis of the pure heart as a high standard. Because of this tradition, strong church communities were built in the past. We, as clergy and lay persons, can revitalize those same small town and rural churches today.

When rural and small town church communities are revitalized, the revival will ripple into our urban and suburban churches. We are all connected as churches and what happens in one part of us affects the other parts. The church will be revived by perfection (sanctification), the kind of Christian example all churches want to offer the people of society. This whole-hearted love of God will appeal to many since it is what they know, deep down, they want and need. God created people with a void in their lives. It remains until they are complete in their relationship with God. As we offer the loving God to men and women, boys and girls, they need to see the living Christ alive in us. The challenge to live truly committed to God is a challenge that will make an impact on the lost. They will pay attention — and respond — if we first practice what we preach.

The spirit of Wesleyan "first love" evangelism, coupled with the principles of Church Growth can provide a powerful answer to the decline of many churches today. We dare not forget, however, that in Revelation 2:5b the church at Ephesus was warned, "Repent and do the things you did at first." So, too, must the modern church repent and return to its first love of evangelism before it can effectively reach large segments of contemporary American society.

Questions for Discussion of Chapter 2

1. What were the positive strengths in the church at Ephesus? What are they in your church?

2. What were the weaknesses in the church at Ephesus? What are they in your church?

3. Explain what it means for a church to "lose its first love."

4. What is unique about the Wesleyan principle of love and how does it relate to your denomination?

5. What is the commitment required for the church to reach large segments of our population today? (Refer to the story of the chicken and the pig.)

Footnotes

[1]Dean M. Kelley, *Why Conservative Churches Are Growing* (San Francisco: Harper and Row, Publishers, Inc., 1977). p. 5.

[2]Kelly, p. 22.

[3]Kelly, pp. 63-64.

[4]Kelly, p. 65.

[5]John Wesley, p. 7.

[6]John Wesley, p. 7.

[7]John Wesley, p. 7.

[8]John Wesley, p. 8.

[9]John Wesley, p. 46.

Chapter 3

A Close Look at Small Town and Rural Churches

The movement of the church into early America was a small town and rural movement. As the first American colonies were established and small communities were organized all over New England, the Christians were there establishing new churches. As the southern United States grew and new towns and villages were founded, the Christians were there establishing new churches. As the Midwest and later the far West opened, the Christians were there establishing new churches. Some of those early villages and towns grew into the large "super-cities" as we know them today. However, most of those early small towns and villages remained relatively small and today there continue to be churches in virtually all of them. In fact, today most of these small towns and villages have an overabundance of churches.

The Early Planting Of New Churches in Every Town and Village

"The earliest Christians met, for most part, in the homes of believers and soon these homes came to be known as "house churches."[1] Paul mentioned some of those house churches in his Epistles (1 Corinthians 16:15; Colossians 4:15; Philemon 2 and Romans 16:4).

The house churches were commonly used by Christians during the first generations of our faith. These places continued until the beginning of the third century excepting, perhaps, in a few of the larger towns. Special buildings for worship did not appear until the close of the second century at which time hall churches were designed to accommodate the larger crowds.

The Christian movement gained its strength for its conquest of the Roman Empire when it was nurtured in small groups of Christians meeting in the homes of believers. In those small groups the believers strengthened each other by their fellowship. They studied together the great truths of their faith. They inspired each other for witnessing and they talked together about what God has done for them.[2]

The eighteenth century revival, which was the beginning of the United Methodist Church in England, was sustained by the class meetings which John Wesley organized. He knew the importance of the meetings as the foundation stones of his new movement. At one time "Wesley stated the values of the class meetings by saying that it could 'scarcely be conceived what advantages had been reaped' from them."[3]

John Wesley realized clearly the spiritual values of personal participation in the worship of small groups."[4] Each participant was accountable to the other participants in the group. Through this commonality the total group had a deep feeling for each individual.

With this background from both the early Christian movement and the early United Methodist Church, the analysis of small town and rural churches can begin. The influence of the early Christian movement and the early Methodist Church upon the growth of other denominations is evident. Every time a new settlement was started on the American frontier, new churches were begun by Methodist circuit riders. As a result, by 1812, the two oldest western states, Kentucky and Tennessee

. . . contained a total Methodist membership of nearly 19,000 while Ohio had two districts, the Miami and the Muskingum, and a membership of more than ten thousand. The whole Western country was now covered with a network of circuits and districts, and the total membership west of the Allegheny Mountains was 30,741 . . .[5]

In 1800, Bishop Asbury had sent out fourteen preachers to take the gospel to the frontiersmen, scattered here and there along the creeks and rivers of the new West; in 1811, Biship McKendue stationed just one hundred preachers at the last session of the Western Conference.[6]

The expansion from fourteen preachers to one hundred preachers in eleven years represents phenomenal growth. The circuit riders were busy about the task of reaching individuals. However, recognizing that these individuals needed nurture, they were quick to appoint leaders among their new converts to start house churches. Consequently, the Methodist Church was able to grow rapidly in its early years. The other denominations also picked up on these same growth concepts.

"From the close of the War of 1812 to 1835 was a period of rapid growth throughout the church."[7] This age was one of restlessness for the country as a whole. In the East new manufacturing towns were springing up in New England and the seaboard states and the constant movement westward meant the beginning of more and more new towns. Everywhere men were working building roads, digging canals and laying tracks for railroads.

> *During the last year (1814) of the War of 1812 there had been an actual decrease of more than three thousand members in the Methodist Episcopal Church, and in 1815 the total increase was but thirty-six; but beginning with 1816, year by year the membership mounted, until in 1833 the increase alone was 51,143, and the total membership had reached the astonishing number of 559,736.*[8]

What a wonderful story to tell! But consider this: suppose the early American church had been sleeping? What if Christians had been unable — or unwilling — to capitalize on these astounding opportunities for new growth on the frontier? The answer is obvious. The church would not have grown and literally tens of thousands of people would not have been won to Christ. However, it is exciting to report that the church leaders were alert — and receptive — to the nudgings of the Holy Spirit; and new preachers were found and the new churches were started.

Where these early churches were not started by class meetings, they were started by the establishment of Sunday church schools. The churches of the Baptist tradition taught the other churches valuable insights into the importance of the establishment of the Sunday church school as a primary source for Church Growth. The strength of those seeds planted in Sunday church schools has continued strong in the Baptist movement even today. The Methodist Church also saw the importance of the Sunday church movement.

At the General Conference of 1824 it was made the duty of each traveling preacher to encourage the establishment and progress of Sunday schools, and arrangements were made for the publication of a catechism for Sunday schools and for the instruction of children.[9]

These Sunday church schools, organized by Methodists, Baptists, and others, were used to reach the children of the community. Once the children were coming, the adult church members began talking to the parents and grandparents of these children.

Based on these great advances, the church continued to advance until the late nineteenth century. The growth was so phenomenal in the Methodist Church that it will be a long time again before it will ever be matched. "It is safe to say that no Christian organization had ever shown such spectacular growth in so short a time."[10] Since the country was still predominantly rural and small-town in nature during this whole period until around the turn of this century, the greatest growth of the church was among the small communities still emerging one-by-one in the rural countryside.

Clearly, small town and rural churches grew because of the impetus — the *passion* — of the early church leaders to plant new churches through class meetings and Sunday church schools. These new churches were planted wherever new settlements were begun.

The Growth of the Small Town and Rural Churches until 1965

Methodist Sunday church school enrollment peaked in 1959. At that time there were almost 7.2 million enrolled. From that year on, Sunday church school enrollment has shown a slow decline. The denomination's membership reached its peak in 1965 with just over eleven million members.[11] Those who have studied church growth and church decline peg the decline of United Methodist Sunday church school enrollment as the first early warning of loss of church membership — which showed up several years later.[12]

The decline in Sunday church school enrollment in the United Methodist Church was attributable to the decline of vigorous church planting. When this vigorous church planting was underway, Sunday church schools grew rapidly. The church was successful in the years following World War II because of this vigorous planting.

Simultaneously, significant shifts have affected America's small and rural areas. The industrial revolution and the movement of masses of people from less populous areas to the urban settings of our country have depersonalized the individual. This has created a certain advantage for — and given a sometimes unrecognized appeal to — small town and rural settings of America where depersonalization has not taken place. Within the small towns strong ties continue between the individual and his or her family, and between the family and the community. The small town and rural church movement put individuals into small groups. This proved consistent — and compatible — with the structure of these communities. Therefore, the class meetings and the Sunday church school classes were accepted by the new converts in such communities because these converts had already been used to small, intimate groups before they became Christians.

Let's take Convoy, Ohio, where the author was pastor from 1973 to 1985 as a case study. In 1875, the town was established. Soon thereafter the circuit riders established a house Sunday church school at a new convert's home. The nucleus grew from that small beginning. Later a small church structure was erected and, in 1915, a large church building was constructed. The dedication and commitment of the early followers, participants in the house Sunday church school, resulted in the growth of the church in Convoy to over three hundred members by 1960. For a town whose population was just over one thousand in 1960, this represents great growth. Countless similar stories could be told of other small towns' church membership growth.

Factors Making Small Town and Rural Churches Unique

In his book, *Why Conservative Churches Are Growing,* Dean M. Kelley identifies methods conservative churches are using in applying Church Growth principles. One of Dr. Kelley's insights is that the leaders of a successful movement are able to get the best out of the followers. He says,

> *The greatest mobilizers, who are usually religious leaders, like John Wesley, are persons who live near their maximum capacity not just for a few moments, but for years — not just for fame or wealth or sport, but for meaning. Is it any wonder that these dedicated, dynamic men and women, intensely and continuously, so much more alive than anyone else, draw to themselves little groups of followers who want to share that abundant life?*[13]

These mobilizers, and the committed groups they lead and inspire, are in every small town and rural church in America. They are the kind of people who, when motivated in the right direction, can make the small town and rural church grow again. It was their kind of leadership which made the church grow in its early history and the small town and rural church can grow again under their leadership today.

> These little bands of committed men and women have an impact on history out of all proportion of their numbers or apparent abilities. In the main, they are usually recruited from the least promising ranks of society; they are not noble or wealthy or well educated or particularly talented. All they have to offer is themselves, but that is more than others give to anything. For when a handful of wholly committed human beings give themselves fully to a great cause or faith, they are virtually irresistible. They cut through the partial and fleeting commitments of the rest of society like a buzz saw through peanut brittle.[14]

From my experience with small town and rural churches, I would have to say that Dean M. Kelley is right on the money. I have found such mobilizing leaders in the ranks of my own pastorate. In the more than fifty churches with which I have come in contact in Church Growth seminars I have met several mobilizing leaders.

In the Scriptures these mobilizing leaders — these individuals for a cause — were the energizers both of the Old Testament Israelites and the New Testament churches. For example, when Jesus selected the twelve disciples, he selected down-to-earth men who were potential motivators. They were not the religious leaders of the land, but were instead uneducated men God ordained, men who then became the great religious leaders of history. These were God's motivators.

Motivators who draw the best out of their followers are able to do so for several reasons.

> (1) They are willing to put in more time and effort for their cause than most people do for even their fondest personal ambitions. (2) They have an assurance, a conviction of rightness, of being on the side of God, that most people in most human endeavors cannot match. (3) They are linked together in a band of mutually supportive, like-minded, equally devoted fellow believers, who reinforce one another in times of weakness, persecution, and doubt. (4) They are willing to subordinate their personal desires and ambitions to the shared goals of the group.[15]

52

The small town and rural churches have mobilizing-leadership potential in their membership. This writer lays a challenge before them: *show* the willingness to give the time needed, to firm up convictions, to band together, and to work with energy on the shared goals of Church Growth. Such potential leadership dare no longer be allowed to sit back and feel sorry for themselves because they are "in nonproductive areas of the country with only a minimal number of people." The mobilizers have unique, qualifying characteristics for potential growth within themselves, *no matter what the obstacles.*

Dean R. Hoge has studied Dean M. Kelley's theories on motivation. Hoge offers some helpful insights based on Kelley's thinking on motivation and Church Growth. Hoge addresses the question of why denominations grow or decline.

> *Kelley's book has been central in recent discussions of denominational trends. His main argument is that churches can be "strong" or "weak." Strong churches (denominations or congregations) grow, while weak ones decline. Strong churches are characterized by (1) a demand for high commitment from their members, including total loyalty and social solidarity. They (2) exact discipline over both beliefs and life-style. They (3) have missionary zeal, with an eagerness to tell the good news to all persons. They (4) are absolutistic about beliefs. Their beliefs area a total, closed system, sufficient for all purposes, needing no revision and permitting none. They (5) require conformity in life-style, often involving certain avoidances of nonmembers through use of distinctinve visible marks or uniforms.16*

Kelley lists what he sees to be the characteristics of weak non-growing churches. He faults the pluralism popular in many of the mainline denominations, seeing it as weakness. Signs of this pluralism are relativism and individualism in beliefs, tolerance, internal diversity, lack of enforcement of canons or doctrines, dialogue with outsiders, limited commitment to church, and little sharing of spiritual insights among the inside group.[17] These traits, Kelley argues, are the signs of a weak church.

If our denominations — and our congregations — display a failure of nerve, a lack of will, an uncertainty about the gospel, a disbelief in the power we have in Jesus Christ; if we have nothing significant to share with one another and with those beyond our

53

church doors; if we have nothing life-changing to offer the world around us because our own lives have not been changed; then our denominations and our congregations will not — and do not deserve to — grow.

To the degree Dean Kelley is right, we had better sit up and listen. To the degree he is right about what makes for strong church life and ministry, we ignore what he has to say to us at our own peril.

Kelley's theorizing is concerned almost entirely with institutional characteristics, not social or historical context or anything external. He says that, "other things being equal," strong churches will grow and weak churches will diminish in numbers.[18]

Small town and rural churches can grow. Convoy, Ohio, United Methodist Church is typical of small town churches. Permit me to refer again to this, my former congregation. The Convoy church is an example of how enabling a potentially capable leadership then inspired the total congregation to apply Church Growth principles — with significant results.

At the time of my appointment to the Convoy church in 1973, the leadership was enthusiastic about having me as their pastor. They wanted me to be involved in the community, to call on the bereaved and the sick, to mingle with the townspeople, to identify with the town's problems, and to lead in worship every Sunday. They would have been satisfied with my doing those things, as long as the financial commitments of the church were met and enough people showed up at worship each week to guarantee a "good crowd." These expectations doubtless describe the mindset of church leaders of typical small town and rural churches all across America.

However, a few of our small town and rural churches have accepted a new challenge and they are growing. The Convoy church accepted a new challenge to grow. The challenge was laid before them Sunday after Sunday, Bible Study after Bible Study, at meeting after meeting, over a period of several years.

As I was inspired by George Hunter, C. Peter Wagner and other Church Growth leaders, I shared that challenge with the congregation. Our church began to change and the growth was dramatic.

Because Church Growth worked for us, a typical small town church, I am convinced it can work for all small town and rural churches whose members are willing to pay the price of risk. The risk we took was to step out financially. The challenge came from good leadership. The leadership laid the challenge properly before the congregation. The result was a favorable vote of eighty-seven percent of the congregation to adopt a proposal to construct a $320,000 addition to the original church building. This addition was clearly needed in order to meet the challenge of growth. The financial commitment was made by corporate faith. Today $250,000 of the original $320,000 is already paid. This amount is on top of a growing, regular budget and a great increase of mission giving.

Church Growth takes hard work. Nevertheless, when the leadership is properly motivated, it can in turn motivate the congretaion to do great things with — and for — God. Until I left the Convoy church in 1985, I was able to tell the congregation each year that we were having our best year yet in finances, attendance in church and Sunday church school, outreach to the community, new commitments to Christ and spiritual vitality. My last year there, 1984, was our best year and it proved by far to have been the greatest increase in five years in every category. Evidence of this increase can be seen in the chart on page 146.

I have taken this challenge to fifty other congregations' leadership, in order to challenge them with the promise that they, too, can grow. All fifty of these churches are in small town and rural communities. All can and will grow if they study themselves, identify the unique factors within their churches which offer them potential for strength instead of weakness, and begin to implement church growth principles.

My challenge is also to you, the reader of this book. Take these concepts into the leadership meetings of your church and begin applying them. Your Administrative Board and/or your Council on Ministries (or whatever equivalent applies for you) will accept this challenge if they are properly motivated.

Let us turn now, in Chapter Four, to the homogeneous unit principle, and see how it applies to your small town or rural church.

Questions for Discussion of Chapter 3

1. What methods were used for planting new churches in the first century church?

2. What methods used for planting new congregations in the early church can be applied to church planting today?

3. What have been the major causes of mainline church decline in the past twenty years?

4. List some factors that make small town and rural churches unique?

56

Footnotes

[1]Curry W. Mavis, *Advancing The Smaller Church* (Grand Rapids: Baker, 1968) p. 13.

[2]*Ibid.*, pp. 13-14.

[3]*Ibid.*, p. 15.

[4]*Ibid.*, p. 26.

[5]William Warren Sweet, *Methodism in American History* (Nashville:Abingdon Press, 1953), p. 165.

[6]*Ibid.*, p. 165.

[7]*Ibid.*, p. 176.

[8]*Ibid.*, pp. 176-177.

[9]*Ibid.*, p. 227.

[10]*Ibid.*, p. 334.

[11]Kelley, p. 5.

[12]Kelley, p. 6.

[13]Kelley, p. 51.

[14]*Ibid.*, p. 51.

[15]*Ibid.*, p. 51.

[16]Dean R. Hoge and David A. Roozen, *Understanding Church Growth and Decline: 1950-1978.* (New York: The Pilgrim Press, 1979). pp. 179-180.

[17]*Ibid.*, p. 180.

[18]*Ibid.*, p. 180.

Chapter 4

Applying The Homogeneous Unit Principle to Small Town and Rural Churches

The homogeneous unit principle is a principle which needs to be understood by small town and rural churches. Basically it means that people tend to be with people who are like themselves. In *Understanding Church Growth,* Dr. Donald McGavran says "The Homogeneous Unit is simply a section of society in which all the members have some characteristics in common. Thus a homogeneous unit (or HU, as it is called in church growth jargon) might be a political unit or subunit, the characteristic in common being that all members live within certain geographical confines."[1]

People like to be and are most comfortable with people who talk, dress, act, and possess things in common to them. Therefore, the Church Growth movement says we can most effectively reach those kinds of people who are like us. For example, farmers can likely reach farmers better than medical doctors can reach farmers. Young couples with children can most effectively reach other young couples with children. We can most effectively reach those of the same or similar socio-economic class. The Church Growth movement says we must reach those like ourselves because the task of evangelism is so large and difficult that by reaching those who are compatible to us, we can be successful in Church Growth.

In this chapter the homogeneous unit principle will be examined as applied to small town and rural churches. In order to accomplish this, let us first look at the practice of the homogeneous unit principle by the United Methodist Church in its early growth. Then we'll look at the biblical basis for the homogeneous unit principle. Next, we will apply the homogeneous unit principle to the modern church. Finally, we will deal with the criticisms of the homogeneous unit principle.

The Practice of the Homogeneous Unit Principle by the United Methodist Church In Its Early Beginnings

The practice of the homogeneous unit principle comes out of the ingrained sociological makeup of *Homo-sapiens*. The individual person is a social creature by nature. In Genesis 1:26-28, the story of the creation of man and woman unfolds. God made these creatures after the likeness of the Godhead (Genesis 1:26) "and God said, Let us make man in our image, after our likeness; and let them have dominion . . ." (Genesis 1:26a) God is social and his creation of humans was that humans be like God and the heavenly beings. Human beings have always striven to be with other human beings. Social contact has been the energizing power behind people's movements from the creation to the twentieth century. The early United Methodist Church understood and used social associations in order to establish and build churches.

The early leaders of the United Methodist Church understood that individuals are not happy alone. John Donne wrote, "No man is an island." Individuals need and want to be with other individuals. For the same reason people marry and establish families. The modern-day proverb that two can live more cheaply than one becomes more relevant with each passing generation.

The sociological grouping of peoples is a universal phenomenon. Dr. McGavran realized this fact as he studied churches across many continents for over twenty years prior to his becoming nationally renowned as the founder of the Church Growth movement. Dr. McGavran says,

> *The people movement mode . . . taking the church into each tribe or caste and letting it grow there . . . is the natural system for India. Men and women become Christian with no feeling of betraying their own people; instead they feel they are benefiting them. Multi-individual conversion will keep the church growing in sufficient strength to affect sizable populations and bring the blessings of the Christian religion, active dependence on Christ, and guidance by His Holy Spirit, to tens of thousands of communities.*[2]

People movements are integral to understanding Church Growth with the use of the homogeneous unit principle. Reaching peoples and people movements proves to be practical. The stumbling block, however, can be the temptation to see peoples as a group instead of seeing humans who individually need a Savior. In effective evangelism this stumbling block must constantly be avoided by evangelists, so that both group dynamics and individual concern may be applied.

In *Understanding Church Growth,* Dr. McGavran begins his Chapter Ten, "Social Structure and Church Growth," with two crucial paragraphs:

> Since church growth takes place in the multitudinous societies of mankind, essential to understanding it is an understanding of their structure. Men exist not as discrete individuals, but as interconnected members of some society. Innovation and social change, operating in particular structures, play a significant part in determining the direction, speed, and size of the move to the Christian religion.
>
> The normal man is not an isolated unit but part of the whole which makes him what he is. For instance, the individual does not choose what language he will speak. The society in which he is born, the mother who nurses him, and the children with whom he plays determine it. Moreover, society either determines or strongly influences every aspect of what he says, thinks, and does. Consequently when we comprehend the social structure of a particular segment of the total population, we know better how churches are likely to increase and ramify through it.[3]

The Church Growth practitioner understands the dynamics of winning groups of people. One key person in a people movement can bring the whole movement to Christ. A person wants to be "in" with his or her group. If the whole group begins moving toward Christ, every individual desires to be a part of that movement because it is what everyone else is doing. Our children use this kind of reasoning when they ask to be a part of an outing or a fad. "But, Mom and Dad, they say, "you just *have* to let me do it; *everyone else* is doing it." This kind of reasoning makes good sense for children. It also makes good sense in Church Growth. It is practical to want to be a part of the group. The flip-side, of course, is that the devil is also aware of this sociological reality. He says, "Everyone else is following me, why not you." Just because the devil has corrupted a good concept, however, there is no need for us to stop using it in its proper perspective, and with God-pleasing results.

The United Methodist Church employed the homogeneous unit principle in its early growth. From the outset it was a people movement. John Wesley was an evangelist to the working classes of England. He was able to win large masses of people to Christ, but the masses he won were found in the working classes. When his circuit riders arrived in America, they also worked with basically one group of people. They reached out to the struggling settlers who were slowly expanding the frontiers of America. They were a homogeneous people. The ingenious way the Holy Spirit used the circuit riders to win these settlers could only have been inspired by God.

> *It is no exaggeration to say that the most significant single factor in the history of the United States has been the Western movement of population, and the churches which devised the best methods for following the population as it pushed westward were the ones destined to become the great American churches. The Methodist Episcopal Church is one of the two largest Protestant churches in the United States today largely because it possessed, or developed, the best technique for following and ministering to a moving and restless population. "It alone was organized as to be able to follow step by step this movable population, and to carry the gospel even to the most distant cabin. It alone could be present whenever a grave was opened, or an infant was found in its cradle.'"[4]*

Thus, we can see that the growth of the United Methodist Church in its early years was in part attributable to the practice of the homogeneous unit principle. Wesley and his followers did not use the present day terminology, but they most definitely understood its practice. Small town and rural churches can apply that biblical principle to reach their communities for Christ today as the early United Methodist Church did. Whatever your denominational affiliation, this Church Growth principle can work for you.

The Biblical Basis for the Homogenous Unit Principle

The homogenous unit principle is biblically grounded. The principle is historically founded in the biblical narrative. Throughout Scripture, the homogeneous unit principle is seen as an interwoven thread of truth. The theological application of this great principle makes the finished product, called "discipleship," complete.

The biblical account of the homogeneous unit principle has always included the emphasis upon one's neighbor. We are to love our neighbors. Until recently, the modern-day concept of "neighbors" in America, meant anyone in your neighborhood. Across America, since World War II, neighborhoods have included homes, a school, some churches, a neighborhood center for recreation and a shopping center. Almost always these "neighborhoods" have been gatherings of people who had at least one or two things in common. They were homogeneous units. Since that time, the rise of apartment buildings and the even newer condominium and trailer or mobile home villages have developed. Once again, they have been the gathering of similar people. National Boards of several denominations are starting congregations where these people are grouped. National Boards of the Baptists and the United Methodists are compiling research at this time for evangelizing homogeneous units in apartment buildings, condominiums, trailer and mobile home villages. The Southern Baptists are evangelizing these homogeneous units to start new churches all over the country. When we reach these homogeneous units we are reaching our neighbor.

The biblical account also emphasizes we are to love our neighbor. These communities that dot our landscape are filled with non-Christians who are much like their Christian neighbors. As the small town and rural church reaches out in love to its neighbor, the gospel proclamation is carried through unto fruition. Carl G. Kromminga in his book *Bringing God's News to Neighbors*, emphasizes these biblical foundations. Dr. Kromminga says, "If this is to be clear even in public greetings, it surely follows that love must be demonstrated in every aspect of one's relationship to the neighbor, whoever he may be."[5] Mr. Kromminga further underscores the importance of loving your neighbor by the following.

> The command of Jesus given in the law of the kingdom is reiterated in the New Testament epistles. Love "keeps no score of wrongs" (N.E.B.) and does not rejoice in unrighteousness but rejoices with the truth (A.S.V.), 1 Corinthians 13:5-6. After admonishing the Corinthians to be watchful and strong in the faith, Paul gives the general injunction, "Let all that you do be done in love," 1 Corinthians 16:14. In Romans 12 Paul deals extensively with the demands of love as they relate not only to fellow believers but also to those outside the church.[6]

God wants small town and rural churches to be ready to help their neighbors whether they are in need or not. Our duty as small town and rural churches is to reach out to those around us.

> *The New Testament repeatedly motivates Christians to reach out to others in a missionary fashion by challenging Christians to reflect on their own experience of God's mercy in Christ. It is this love which Christ has for Paul which prompts him to be of service to others. (1 Corinthians 5:14) Although the apostles and not the church as a whole directly received the command to evangelize the nations, congregations do share a driving motive for missions born of their experience of God's free mercy and grace in Christ. According to the pattern already laid down in the Old Testament, in the New Testament era God displays his grace in and to the church and via the church God reaches the heathen.*[7]

Our love for our neighbor must be deeply embedded in the biblical truth that without Christ that neighbor is lost and doomed forever. Without Christ he is in spiritual darkness, and it is our love for him that drives us to him with great desire to rescue him from sin and from eternal punishment. Therefore, in this love for our neighbor we see judgment. The judgment is not ours, but God's. We are not to act superior to our neighbor because we have something that makes us better than he is. No, it is only by God's grace that we have anything. And in and through Christ and his love we share his love with our neighbors.

Therefore, in the biblical account the emphasis upon the homogeneous unit is seen in the admonition to love our neighbor. Modern society is structured in a way that will enhance the gospel mandate. Those people who are outside the faith in our communities are the ones we can and should reach. Church history has proven that many churches have been started in communities and grown into great churches because the people first won in those churches have faithfully reached their neighbors. Those neighbors have by and large been people of their same homogeneous unit. Thus the historical biblical gospel has been carried out through a simple concept which is ingrained in humanity's essential character.

Still another biblical account refers to the homogeneous unit principle. Unique to the history of the world were the chosen people of ancient days called Hebrews. These people were both culturally and religiously unique in the ancient world because their culture and religion were so intertwined. However, their most salient characteristic was their claim to be God's chosen people. Because of their claim, and the implications of it, their struggle has been very difficult. These people of the Old Testament, called Jews, (since the Babylonian captivity) have held onto their identity down to the present age. The homogeneous unit principle runs deep into their culture and religion. They were and still are a homogeneous unit. It must be noted, however, that these people were culturally and even somewhat religiously diverse. Within their culture, as within most cultures in the history of the world, have been many subcultures.

To be a Jew in the Old Testament times was to be a follower of the great Yahweh. Because of the dedication of these people, their unity was evident. They drew the interest of many other people. Some groups hated them and were deeply jealous of these people called Jews. This strife caused many wars which are recorded in the Old Testament. Others were enthralled by them and sought their blessings and favor. Still others tried to emulate the Jews. Of this group there was a strong desire to belong to the Jews, or better yet, to become Jewish. For a non-Jew to become a Jew was difficult. The importance of being born a Jew and having Jewish blood was supreme. In his book *Evangelism in the Early Church,* Michael Green writes about the problems faced by God-fearers and proselytes.

> But the very graduation of Jews, proselytes, God-fearers and plain Gentiles was an indirect preparation for the Gospel. For no man could be a "son of Abraham" in the fullest sense unless he was born a Jew. The Mishna says that the proselyte should pray in synagogue. "O God of your fathers," he is not, and never can be, on a par with them. Indeed, even the Jew of the Dispersion sank in status when he was out of the Holy Land, for there were some points of his religion, notably sacrifice, which he could not carry out. Women and children, too, were less than full citizens of Israel, at least in the sight of the Jewish male, who thanked God daily that he was not born a woman! All such class distinction was done away within Christianity, and this gave the new religion a flying start on Roman soil; after all, however much he admired the Jewish religion and ethics, it was hard for a Roman citizen to demean himself by becoming a second class citizen of a despised and captive Oriental nation. But this was not necessary in order to become a Christian, where all men were brothers, and distinctions of race, sex, education, and wealth meant nothing.[8]

Thus, we can see that the Old Testament Jews were a somewhat closed homogeneous unit. They, by virtue of their beliefs, were unable to fully accept outsiders. This in itself made the possibility of Church Growth very difficult indeed. The distinction between a Jewish and a non-Jewish believer, as highlighted by Dr. Green, was very marked. Two of the laws which Christianity erased, making it much easier for Gentiles to accept Christianity, were the dietary laws and circumcision. The replacement of circumcision by baptism made Christianity appealing to non-Jews.

Since the Old Testament chosen people people were a homogeneous unit, it would seem they would have been able to use this fact to win the lost to the chosen race. But because of already-mentioned obstacles, the task was almost impossible. The Jewish people were not able to reach others effectively because their homogeneous unit was structured in such a way that others who tried to come into the unit were never placed on the same level as the Jews who were born into their faith. As Michael Green says, "They were second class citizens."

The sort of homogeneous unit which the Jews were, made the activation of the homogeneous unit principle impossible. They were zealous at winning proselytes to their faith, but the proselytes were never able to lead the church. We have a similar problem in some evangelism today. Some missionaries and evangelists enthusiastically go out to win the lost, only to then separate the newly-saved from the home-based group because they are not culturally or linguistically the same. Thus, these new converts sense their second-class citizenship and are never part of the end group. Still, God is able to work through — and in spite of — this wrongly-based evangelism and mission work just as he did in the ancient days of Judaism to bring the proselytes to his faith.

We also have a similar problem with our small town and rural churches. These churches, too, are homogenous units. The leaders of these churches, who many times are zealous at reaching new people, want new members. However, the new people never really feel fully part of the group because the membership is so close-knit. Outsiders are not able to break the barrier. If the new people are welcomed into the church, they have much difficulty as the years pass because they are never asked to lead the church. The unspoken rule among long-time members is that they are the leaders and the newcomers are the followers. Thus these newcomers are second class citizens, just as were the proselytes in the Old Testament Jewish community.

Dr. Green again:

> *What spurred them to this missionary endeavour? Paradoxically, it was their exclusivism. The more seriously one believed (and men did believe Antiochus Epiphanes onwards) that Israel was what mattered to God, while the nations were, as the writer of* 2 Esdras *engagingly puts it, "like unto spittle," the more one was bound to try to rescue some brands from the burning. We then have a chain reaction. Persecution led the Jews along the paths of apocalyptic, according to which, in the coming Messianic Kingdom, all wrongs would be righted, Israel would be vindicated, and the ungodly Gentiles crushed. This in turn led to proselytizing, for one could not with an easy conscience reflect on the fewness of the saved and the multitudes of the lost and do nothing about it. Hence the growing concern to bring Gentiles under the wing of the people of God.* [9]

To make this evangelism work, the divine providence of God had to be involved, for by the time of Christ there were numerous groups of believers who were proselytes, God-fearers, Hellenists and others placed all around the world of that day. These non-Jews were turning to the one and only God of the Jews in large numbers because of the vigouous evangelization of many faithful and concerned Jews. Yet they were never full-fledged members of the Jewish church. Many scholars feel this was God's way of preparing for the coming of the Jewish Messiah. When Christ came, he had audiences from many groups other than Jews because of their previous interest and their commitment to the one and only true God of the Jews. Thus, in all reality, God was able to use the homogeneous unit principle to reach many groups of people when the Messiah came. Therefore, as the homogeneous unit principle had been a hindrance in the case of Jewish proselytes, it was, on the other hand, highly effective in reaching these proselytes — God-fearers, Hellenists and others across the Roman Empire, for Christianity. In fact, the Jews as a group were unable to accept Christ even though he was born a Jew and was proclaimed prior to his actual coming as the Messiah. The problem these Israelites had with Christ was that his message was too radical and his acceptance of the non-Jews was unconditional. They, therefore, as a group rejected the very one for whom they had waited with anticipation. On the other hand the non-Jewish groups came readily to acceptance of Christ.

One of the age-old problems of the homogeneous unit principle surfaced in the life of the Old Testament chosen people. They saw the need for reaching the lost. They won the lost; yet they did not allow the lost full status, for their homogeneous unit was closed to outsiders. The outsiders they won, by the divine grace of God, accepted their faith even with its second class status. Then when new revelation came in the person of Christ, they much more readily accepted him *while the closed homogeneous unit rejected him.*

I believe a parallel can be drawn to the western evangelization of the third world in the past century, up to the present. The missionaries of the West have vigorously won the "pagans of the jungles." Those new pagan converts have remained second-class citizens of the faith, except when they have become truly westernized. They have accepted Christ *in spite of* second-class status. Now the stories coming to the West tell of great revivals surging in the third world. A new revelation of the Holy Spirit is spreading rapidly among the second-class believers. Yet those of us in the Western churches tend to downplay and not accept the new movement of the Holy Spirit. We have rejected the new coming of the Holy Spirit, just as the Jews rejected the Messiah. Thus the homogeneous unit concept can stifle the work of God, as both Old Testament and present-day experiences point out.

Later in this chapter we will discuss the criticisms of the homogeneous unit principle. However, the criticism of ethnicity which has been alluded to in our current discussion of the Old Testament Jews needs examination at this point. The question must be asked: "Is ethnicity a sin?" The answer is an obvious "No." The problem lies with how one ethnic group or homogeneous unit treats another ethnic group. The Jews could only see themselves being (authentic) Jews. Others could believe in their (Jewish) God but they were second-class citizens. This is not so with God. In the creation he made man and woman. He was not a respector of persons. All people were created in God's image: this guaranteed a unity among them. People were created social beings and God created a common thread of social acceptability and worth in all. From the beginning a sociological phenomenon called cultural diversity existed. God made people culturally diverse, but in the Creator's eyes all have equal status. People have struggled with cultural diversity since the creation. Individuals have said. "Yes, cultures are different. There are other cultures other than mine, but mine is superior." Cultural divisions came. Thus cultural status and roles were developed and there were the "have's" and the "have not's." This was due to original sin. When a person considers his or her group or culture is better or superior to other groups or cultures, he or she sins. God tried to intervene with the Israelites to correct the cultural division which was as wrong as that of the pagans around them. The cultural division issue among the Israelites eventually caused much conflict, enmity, and strife between the Northern Kingdom and the Southern Kingdom are examples which Dr. Arthur Glasser lifted up for members of the Church Growth II class I attended while at Fuller Seminary in August of 1981.

Dr. Glasser said then that unity within cultural diversity was the main ingredient. This unity within cultural diversity is called cultural pluralism. Cultural pluralism is what the Messiah brought when he arrived. He was able to unite Jews and Gentiles alike with the message of unity within cultural diversity. The acceptance of cultural pluralism is our answer today. The people of God can be united and equal in their faith in God even though they are culturally diverse. The homogeneous unit principle will work when this fact is understood and accepted. Small town and rural churches need to understand cultural pluralism. Even in a small town community or a rural setting several homogeneous units exist. These diverse groups of people can be reached when the small town and rural church understands them as *different cultural groups or homogeneous units.* Once they are understood as groups, the church can either reach one of these groups as a homogeneous unit within the framework of the church or there can be started a new church in the community for a particular cultural group.

The homogeneous unit principle in the New Testament account is seen in Jesus' cultural sensitivity. He was sensitive to all cultural groups in his ministry. His Jewish critics were upset when he associated with tax collectors and sinners. Jesus' sensitivity was deeply imbedded within the framework of what God had planned before the beginning of time — and what he tried to develop in the Old Testament believers. The early church followed the example of Jesus. The teachings of the apostles emphasized the unity yet diversity of the believers.

The New Testament tells of the first people movement. On the day of Pentecost, three thousand Jews came to believe in Jesus as Messiah and Lord. They were baptized. They received the Holy Spirit. They continued in the apostles' teaching and fellowship, in the breaking of bread and the prayers. Yet they did not cease to be Jews. They continued going to the Temple. They maintained the taboo against pork. They continued to circumcize their male babies on the eighth day. They observed the Sabbath, and refused to eat with Gentiles. They continued to take pride in the fact that they were of the tribe of Benjamin, or Judah, or Levi; continued to marry their sons to Jewish girls of the right subtribe and to enter into all the contractual relationships which that entailed. Their weddings were undoubtedly solemnized by Jewish rituals.[10]

Just as the Jews kept many of their rituals and customs, so it is right for Gentiles to bring into their new-found faith many components of their former culture. Retaining cultural identity and living the Christian life were part of the unity and diversity of the early church. By allowing people of other cultures to retain characteristics of those cultures in their new-found faith, the apostles were establishing the homogeneous unit principle as a basic principle of Church Growth.

Tribe is another term which is used to identify the homogeneous unit. Dr. McGavran indicates the failure of the missionary effort in the past few hundred years to understand the *tribe* or people movement. He affirms the Church Growth emphasis on winning the tribes, the nations and the peoples. He reminds us that the first ten chapters of Acts are an indication of the validity of this method. These chapters mention several examples of multitudes being won to Christ:

In my earlier volume, The Bridges of God, *Chapter III illustrated the people movement from the New Testament. I wrote that chapter not to prove from the Bible that people movements are right, but simply because the New Testament affords a good example of a people movement.*[11]

Dr. McGavran continues:

When once the tight caste structure of the Jewish community of our Lord's day has been realized, it is impossible to miss the people movement nature of New Testament church growth. The journeys of St. Paul also, far from being like those of the modern mission- ary, are typical of the way in which a movement expanding in a sin- gle urban caste or rural tribe follows the line of relations and the natural connections of one family with another.[12]

Dr. McGavran illustrates with the example of Acts 17:10-14. In this account the whole synagogue community in Beroea turned to Christ, reorganized and became a Christian church in just a few days. "Here it is sufficient to call attention to the fact that if the Holy Spirit guided the early church to grow in people-movement fashion, there cannot be any inherent wrong in it. Here my plea is simply that a kind of church growth which occurs in people-conscious societies is right and biblical."[13]

If winning tribes or groups to Christ is biblical, and I feel Dr. McGavran is correct in his belief that it is, then what about our one- ness in Christ in relation to the homogeneous unit principle. Dr. Richard R. De Ridder alludes to this in his book, *Discipling the Na- tions.* We are one in Christ Dr. De Ridder says.

The New Testament shows most clearly that there is a oneness in Christ that breaks down every political, social, racial, moral, sexual barrier. The oneness of Jew and Greek, slave and free man, male and female is found in and guaranteed in Christ (Galatians 3:26-28); excluded in Christ are such divisions as circumcised and uncircum- cised, barbarian, Scythian (Colossians 3:11). This is the develop- ment that should be expected on the basis of God's universal covenant. The purpose of God is to unite all things in Christ; this is his plan for the ages (Ephesians 1:9-10). When we are told that "the dividing wall of hostility" has been broken down (Ephesians 2:14), this means that Jesus Christ has something to say about and to do with and toward whatever divisions exist in our society: the differences between races, nations, people. Jesus Christ has broken down every barrier, division, and frontier between men. But that is most wonderful of all — he has reconciled men to God.[14]

Dr. De Ridder's point is clear: no person can claim Christ exclu- sively. Christ abolishes segregation, for there is no separation due to color of skin, difference of age, sex or language. We cannot separate any part of our life from Christ.

On the one hand, this oneness in Christ seems to contradict the homogeneous unit principle. On the other hand, it supports the principle. If we are one in Christ, we have unity. Yet we are culturally different from one another. Therefore, we find our unity in Christ in our appreciation for our diversity. The prime example of this is seen in our hundreds of denominations within the Christian church. Most of our denominational differences are cultural. Yet we have a strong unity in the centrality of Jesus Christ. Most denominations in the United States have regional sections which are homogeneous units. Some of the smaller more regionally-oriented denominations are entirely one homogeneous unit. My friend, Dr. Herbert Carter, the General Superintendent of the Pentecostal Free Will Baptist Church, told me that his denomination is made up of one homogeneous unit. It is a regional denomination in the North Carolina mountains. God uses and blesses all of us as we work together for his glory. We are to be one in Christ and united in him; yet culturally we are of many different backgrounds.

Dr. Harry Boer, in his book *Pentecost and Missions,* highlights the apostles' practice of homogeneous unit evangelism through conversion patterns in the family unit. A oneness exists within the family unit, one which God intended from the creation. God created the family concept for mankind. Eve was Adam's helpmate from God. The two were commanded to partner in order to bring unity and offspring. Through the children that were born, a true unit was established. The immediate family and extended family members were united. Reaching this homogeneous unit and bringing them to conversion and discipleship is an approach which was highly successful in the book of Acts.

> *Only let not the great emphasis that Acts places on the family unit in a People Movement to Christ in the context of missionary witness be lost on us as we reflect on the vast importance of social ties in the life of the convert and the Church in which he must live the new life of the Spirit. For, in a unique sense, approaches to a People through the family is its veritable "highway of the spirit."*[15]

Using families as avenues to reach people for Christ is a method which God ordained and intended for winning the lost. This family-type ministry is effective in small town and rural churches. The extended families of any small town or rural church family are open territory for reaching with the gospel.

In his Chapter VIII, "Pentecost and the Witnessing Church in Action," where Dr. Boer is discussing the family as a group to evangelize, he points to the need for witnessing. Because the Lord wants the church to witness, the church is compelled to witness. It is God's will the church be a witnessing church. Hence, the true church is a mission church. Missions and the church are one in the same. Dr. Boer used the book of Acts to clarify his understanding of what the church really is.

Boer refers extensively to Donald McGavran's "people movement," concept. Like other critiques of this concept called "people movements," Dr. Boer wants to be careful about people movements. The personal gospel is so essential that "people movements" can miss the individuals within the movement.

The small town and rural churches have been people movements. The growth of our small town and rural churches in past years can be attributed to the reaching of whole families for Christ. McGavran calls these kinds of movements "highways of the Spirit" because the Holy Spirit is able to work through one member of the family to touch other members of the family and win them to Christ.

Thus, the people movement becomes exceptionally effective when the family which is converted reaches out *to the extended family*. In the study of people movements Dr. McGavran found strong connections between the family and the extended family. Where this has been understood by evangelists, large groups of extended families have been reached. In turn, those of the extended families have reached other groups of *their* extended families and the results have been phenomenal. Dr. McGavran calls this approach evangelism through "family webs."

However, there are also other webs. The social network or web between groups of people is an effective approach to evangelism. The house congregation was most effective in that regard in the early church. Those who have done research on the first century church tell us that it was the house church which instituted the thriving church of the first century.

Not until the year A.D. 120 or thereabouts was the first church *building* constructed. Therefore, the church thrived for more than one century without a building. In our building-conscious society today, this almost seems impossible. Professor John Wimber (mentioned later in this chapter), saw his congregation grow from zero to over 3,000 worshipers each Sunday in just a few years. That's an example of what can happen without even having a building. The first century church was able to accomplish the task with brick and morter.

One may see the homogeneous unit principle at work through the unity of the people of God. Wherever one goes as a Christian, one can instantly be one with a stranger who is a Christian because of the oneness shared in Christ. Moreover, this unity which was the force behind the church is witnessed in the Old and New Testaments. The power of the Holy Spirit is the source of this thread of unity. Thus, the homogeneous unit principle is a powerful tool for winning the lost. In the Old and New Testaments the people of God used this power to bring outsiders to the inside of the faith.

The Application of the Homogeneous Unit Principle Today

In order to make proper application of the homogeneous unit principle today we can first look to the historical struggle of people. Historically humanity has struggled with self identity. Everyone has to come to the point in their life when they ask, "Who am I, where did I come from, and where am I going?" In the twentieth century people are still asking these same questions. George E. Ladd in his book, *The Gospel of the Kingdom* alludes to our dilemma:

> *In a day like this, wonderful yet fearful, men are asking questions. What does it all mean? Where are we going? What is the meaning and the goal of human history?*[16]

The question further asked is, Do we have a destiny? As we struggle in our society with who we are and where we are going, we are struggling with some of the most difficult questions we can ask. The answers to those questions are found in the gospel of the kingdom of God. We Christians can reach the age in which we live if we are available when the people are asking the questions. We have the answers they need, but they will not find the answers unless they ask the right questions. When they ask the right questions, we are ready to provide the right answers.

The kingdom of God is the answer to our dilemma. The kingdom of God is in Christ Jesus. He is the hope of all and in all. When people start asking the right questions, we have the answers. Dr.

Ladd's book puts the answers in proper perspective.

The biblical foundation for human identity is focused on the coming of the person who was God. This historical event, when people and God were united in human flesh, is the biblical foundation for the answer to people's search for identity and truth.

Those of us who call ourselves evangelists must understand the searchings of people to find God. Francis Thompson's epic poem *The Hound of Heaven* puts this search in reverse perspective. It is God who seeks out the individual until he finds him. The individual runs from God but no matter where the individual goes or where he tries to hide, God finds him. We cannot hide from God. Both approaches are biblically based and historically founded. People *do* run from God; yet in their running they are actually *seeking* God.

Permit me to share my own personal quest for God. At the age of nineteen, I left home to join the United States Air Force — to remove myself from my church, my family, and many good, praying people. God had called me to preach when I was ten years old. Yet I was running from him. Much to my surprise, God was in the United States Air Force. He was there waiting for me with outstretched arms. I reached out for those arms and they embraced me. I found what I was looking for by running from what I did not want. Yet what I found was what I was running from. I found in Christ the meaning of history. I found in him the meaning of *my* history.

Yet, the point that needs to be made is that the homogeneous unit principle was at work. The very people (church, family, and praying people) from whom I was running were really leading me to Christ. Though I was away from them, they were still praying I would find Christ, and down deep within me I was cheering for their prayers because I desperately needed and wanted what they had. My leaving home was a sign to them that what they had, I wanted. They must have sensed my despair, for they prayed harder. Then I was found in Christ. Therefore, it was the homogeneous unit which I respected. Even though I left home I still wanted to belong to the home people.

But is not my story the story of legions? Are we not all alike? Is not the answer, to the lost being found, in the endeavors of those who care, to show that passion to the lost? The answer to all of these questions is a resounding "Yes!" People are searching historically for their identity. Through the love of people who are of the same homogeneous unit, people will listen and, we hope, they will exchange their lost state for one of being found in Christ. Moreover, the small town and rural church is a homogeneous unit. If it can catch hold of its identity as such, its leaders can reach out to people of the community who are like themselves and win some of them to Christ and for the local church. The small town and rural church needs to have a homogeneous unit strategy to reach those like themselves.

Dayton and Fraser, in their books, *Planning Strategies for World Evangelization* discuss this problem of finding the lost who are ready to be found. In their Chapter Thirteen, "Understanding the Behavior of a People," they point to the problem of reaching the lost. They use the Church Growth terms "resistance" and receptivity."

> *Assessing receptivity or resistance to the gospel is basic within a strategy for evangelization. If a people is extremely receptive — like Cornelius, they are ready to believe and only await the words of life — then almost any method or strategy will reap a great harvest. Mistakes will be easily rectified and forgotten, If, on the other hand, a people is strongly resistant to Christian commitment (even assuming a culturally sensitive approach in evangelism), then, in most cases, even the best of strategies will fail.*[17]

(I will discuss resistance and receptivity in detail in Chapter Eight.)

When those of us who believe in evangelism are open to the leading of the Holy Spirit, we are able to reach those people who are receptive within the framework of the homogeneous unit principle. Resistant people will continue to be resistant even to those of the same homogeneous unit until the barriers of their resistance are removed. We must understand this resistance in order not to become unduly discouraged.

Let me once again allude to the small town church where I recently served. The Convoy United Methodist Church was a growing church because we were applying Church Growth principles. Many of these Church Growth principles were actively being used in our congregation in order to prompt growth in our congregation. One of the most effective principles we used was the homogeneous unit principle. This principle *works* in growing churches. God is definitely using it for the growth of that congregation.

Before becoming involved in Church Growth, I spent too much time with "the-world-is-my-parish" concept. The concept is from John Wesley and I had the wrong perception of the concept. The world *is* my parish, and I need to be involved with people whom God leads to me. However, I can only nurture growing churches with people who are of the same homogeneous unit. Many have struggled with this concept, but I have found it to be true. People are attracted to people who are like themselves. Of the seventy-five new families reached, not one of them were any different from the already existing members of the church. We reached receptive people in our community — people like us. Peter Wagner refers to Church Growth founder Dr. Donald McGavran when he discusses this issue.

> *The debate continues and probably will for some time to come, but the issue is clear. The classic statement of the homogeneous unit principle remains McGavran's: "Men like to become Christians without crossing racial, linguistic, or class barriers." Notice that McGavran is focusing here on non-Christians rather than Christians. His purpose in advocating the homogeneous unit principle is consistently that of bringing non-Christians into the Christian movement. An underlying assumption of the principle has always been that once people become Christians and are growing in their application of biblical ethical principles to their daily lives, they will lose their inclinations toward racism and prejudice. This work of grace operates in Christians, but presumably not in the same way in non-Christians. Christians, therefore, are free to group themselves in churches in whatever way they wish along homogeneous or heterogeneous lines. Both are good Christian options, but the decision should be made intelligently, and the consequences of each option weighed.* [18]

I am thankful we understood this concept while I was at the Convoy Church. We loved the people of our community who were not like us, but we were only able to disciple those who were like us.

This illustration of the homogeneous unit principle from my own struggles with Church Growth in the local church setting convinced me its position as a valid Church Growth principle. Its practicality has been validated since its inception as a principle. The studies of the sociological factors of groups and peoples further validates it.

Another example of the use of the homogeneous unit principle comes from Pastor John Wimber and his Calvary Chapel Church in the Los Angeles area. A few years ago John Wimber started a church for the eighteen-to-thirty-year-olds, a segment of the population which no church was reaching. His strategy was to get the attention of the affluent young adults who were turned off to the conventional church. When I heard John Wimber tell his story at Fuller Seminary in August of 1981, his congregation still did not have a church building or facility. They were using rented facilities which they had to change every few months as their congregation kept growing. They had grown from zero to over 3,000 in worship because they were reaching a particular homogeneous unit whom God had laid on their hearts.

We can apply the homogeneous unit principle to our small town and rural churches and win the people of like homogeneous units to Christ. We must first understand the principle, then accept it as valid and finally apply it to our local situations.

Criticisms of the Homogeneous Unit Principle

If the small town and rural church is to grow, it must deal with the criticisms of the homogeneous unit principle. Ever widening debate is developing in the Christian church over the Church Growth movement. On the one side are those who are excited about Church Growth because it is working for them. On the other side, are those who have either tried Church Growth and it has not worked for them, or those who have not tried it and do not want anything to do with it.

Central to Church Growth debate is the issue of the homogeneous unit principle. Church Growth supporters and practitioners know that the homogeneous unit principle is crucial to the process of Church Growth. On the other hand, Church Growth detractors and skeptics are convinced that the homogeneous unit principle is an abomination to the Christian church.

We can frame the debate in four words: Is ethnicity a sin? Dr. Donald McGavran discusses at length the issue of ethnicity. He defends vigorously the reaching of individual ethnic groups. He calls this type of evangelism the reaching of peoples. When we reach groups and they come to Christ, they are called people movements. He asks the question, "Are efforts to missionize people movements soundly Christian? Is it unbiblical to reach out specifically to peoples or tribes?"

These are fair questions. In answer, one should turn directly to the Bible and observe its authority for discipling tribes. At the outset, the whole Old Testament is the story of God's dealings with peoples. God called the Hebrew people, the children of Israel, the twelve tribes, out of Egypt. Again and again He disciplined them as peoples. Again and again they made group decisions, repented of their sins, and convenanted with God to walk in His ways.

Coming to the New Testament, we note that Matthew 28:19 instructs Christians to disciple the tribes. In Hindi, the national language of India, the words read jatiyon ko chela karo, *i.e. "disciple the castes" — a much more accurate rendering of the Greek than the common English version "make disciples of the nations." What our Lord said was precisely "disciple the tribes," the castes and families of mankind. Just as the Jewish tribes were the people of God, so the multitudinous peoples of the Gentiles should become God's household.*[19]

America was founded on the concept of freedom of religion. Our forefathers began this country with a belief and hope that people would gather here from all walks of life and eventually all melt into one culture, one intermixed race. This concept was nicknamed the melting pot theory. America was called the "Melting Pot" of the world's people. History has proved these past two hundred years that though the intentions were good, we are not one people but instead we are still a land of many peoples and many ethnic subcultures.

The United Methodist denomination, for one, has historically stressed the same concept with reference to the gospel. Wesley taught, "The world is my parish." United Methodist ministers and churches have long tried to reach the whole community of which they were a part. This effort has been particularly true with small town and rural churches. However, their efforts have mostly gone fruitless. The churches that have grown have stressed reaching the neighbor and the neighorhood. In changing communities the church has become the people *outside* the community who faithfully commuted weekly to and from the services. Thus, the church has failed to reach the community which lives around the building. The failure is not the failure of the gospel, nor its lack of effectiveness, but rather the failure of one ethnic or cultural group being able to reach another ethnic or cultural group.

It is not a sin to target those most like ourselves and to send missioners who fit better with other cultures to those cultures in order to reach them. God had planned it this way in the beginning. Let us examine this issue from both perspectives and see if the debate over the homogeneous unit principle can be understood and resolved.

The founder of the Church Growth movement, Dr. Donald A. McGavran, has studied churches from all denominations all over the world. He says, "In every land we have congregations not only of different denominations, but of different social structures and differing degrees of tolerance or ostracism — different relationships to and degrees of acceptance by the 'yet to believe'."[20] It is the task of those interested in Church Growth to understand the "ethnic realities," as Dr. McGavran calls them. Dr. McGavran first discovered the reality of ethnic power in his studies and research of churches all around the world in the twenty or more years prior to publishing his *Bridges of God* in 1955. He called this early discovery the homogeneous unit principle. Dr. McGavran says,

> *Since, however, growth is frequently slowed or stopped in the midst of great opportunity because of ethnicity and other sociological factors, I have thought it important to concentrate some attention on these, in a setting where they can be both broadly and coherently examined in relation to the society and also to each other.*[21]

Thus, the homogeneous unit principle is very much related to growth or lack of growth in any given church. Dr. McGavran and Church Growth movement folk believe that churches grow most effectively when they attract people *of the same homogeneous unit*. This is not to say that churches cannot grow unless they seek to bring people of the same homogeneous unit into the church. The point is rather that churches *grow most effectively* when the homogeneous unit is used for all it's worth.

The Church Growth movement does not oppose crossing cultural barriers in order to win the lost. On the contrary, the Church Growth movement expends much time and energy crossing cultural barriers in order to win other people and thus tries to match the proper evangelists culturally with the proper people. The results of this proper matching can be extremely successful as Church Growth research and practice have proven.

On the other side of the homogeneous unit issue are the critics of the Church Growth movement. One evangelical critic of the movement is Mennonite leader, Dr. John H. Yoder. In his questioning of the homogeneous unit, Dr. Yoder asks:

Does the concept of the "homogeneous unit", whose people can respond to the gospel all more or less in the same way, promise to become increasingly helpful and its contents increasingly defined in the development of urban societies, or is it a concept which applies best where there is the least social movement so that its adequacy will decrease with proletarianization, urbanization, and the forming of personality by the mass media? Is the concept of the "homogeneous unit" within which an effective church can mature the way to squeeze the last growth potential out of the tribe past or is it a help to guide us in moving into the urban world of the future? Is the concept of the church "maturing" into domination over a given "homogeneous unit," so that it will grow primarily by biological reproduction, a serious possibility which contemporary sociology can deal with?[22]

Dr. Yoder believes the homogeneous unit principle will hinder growth in urban societies which are growing so rapidly in almost every corner of the world. He and some mainline denomination critics believe the homogeneous unit concept will work only in the small rural societies of the world.

Other critics of the homogeneous unit principle stress that the gospel is not for only one group in a society. These critics say it is sinful to work among one segment of the society while neglecting other segments or people. Many leaders of my own United Methodist denomination struggle with this problem. They stress that the Church Growth movement must spread itself across all segments of a given society in order to reach some.

Perhaps the two sides are not as far apart as one might think. As a Church Growth student, I must admit that the movement is interested in all segments of a given culture. My most recent congregation was interested in reaching all segments of our community. Yet, we were frustrated with the trying. We had found that we could grow best by reaching our own homogeneous unit. The people we were able to draw, win, and disciple were the people who were of our own homogeneous unit. Occasionally, we drew and won people from another unit. However, the results were that these people either through "redemption and lift" moved into our homogeneous unit, or they had to move, eventually, to another church where they were more comfortable. We urged these people to make the move to another church as we were aware they do not fit in with us. We did not fail to win people of other homogeneous units if the opportunity arose. We wanted to win everyone we could possibly win. However, our evangelists felt much more comfortable reaching out to people like themselves. The people like our evangelists felt much more accepting to the evangelists' message.

The critics of the homogeneous unit principle would say that we did not care about others. However, we *did* care — and we tried to work with the culturally different churches in our community. We wanted to support their outreach and, on many occasions, we had led them to receptive peoples who would be much more receptive to them than to our ministry. The answer, of course, is to send out evangelists to each ethnic group in society.

I believe the critics of the movement have not understood it. The use of the homogeneous unit principle is most important to evangelism. The followers of Christ in every century have known its attributes. The early church grew in leaps and bounds because of a fervent desire of the disciples to win the lost.

> *The story of Pentecost is well known. A living organism was created (1 Corinthians 12:12-13) and it soon demonstrated its capacity as a life-communicating presence among men. On that first day its numbers increased by 3,000. The flame went from heart to heart. In the weeks and months that followed, this living Church demonstrated its capacity to reach outward in a spontaneous fashion with the good news of Jesus Christ. In the early chapters of the Acts (2-12) we see evidence of the existing possibilities of what has been termed "near neighbor evangelism." Jerusalem, Judea, Samaria, Galilee — among the people of Palestine the devoted believers reaped the harvest where Jesus and his disciples had earlier sowed the good seed of the gospel of the Kingdom.*[23]

In Dr. Glasser's conclusion to his discussion on mission theology, he said:

> *In those early years the living faith we know as Christianity seemed to grow and reach but without special "methods" for its propagation. It was a lay movement through and through. Its members loved and rejoiced and served and witnessed. And the pagans round about "saw . . . a quality of living, and supremely of dying, which could not be found elsewhere . . . Men will not believe that Christians have good news to share until they find that bishops and bakers, university professors and housewives, bus drivers and street corner*

preachers are all alike keen to pass it on, however different their methods may be (Green, 1970:275). In the end the royal house was penetrated. Even the Emperor Constantine capitulated, and during his reign Christianity not only gained the official recognition of the State, but became the State religion.[24]

The role of the Church Growth movement is the role of evangelism and the growth of churches. The homogeneous unit principle is one of the most important factors for Church Growth. This chapter has only begun to delve into all the aspects of its impact on discipline the nations.

There are critics of the homogeneous unit principle as there are critics of the whole Church Growth movement. John H. Yoder is a critic of the movement. He says he is a firm supporter of Church Growth and I believe he is sincere in his statement. However, he questions the Church Growth movement on many points.

One of the foundations of the movement is the concept "people movements." Mr. Yoder challenges this concept. He asks how the individual gospel works in a "people movement" to Christ. He questions whether individual conversion happens to all the members of the movement when a large group of people come to Christianity.

The books of Acts is the foundation of the people movement theory which Dr. McGavran saw at work in India and elsewhere in the world. I believe it is a valid concept. I have seen it work on a small scale in my own ministry, in my own congregation.

The homogeneous unit principle is both practical and biblical. Human beings are social beings. The logic of and necessity for the principle is evidenced by a study of the sociological makeup of human beings. Historically, in the biblical narrative — both Old Testament and New Testament; from the ancient believers, through the first century church, up to the modern church, the movement of the homogeneous unit principle has proven effective.

The homogeneous unit principle must be understood — and taken seriously — by the small town and rural church if that church is to grow. The understanding of the principle can come by studying the history of planting new churches in every town and village. Understanding can come by studying its biblical basis. The homogeneous unit principle will work in the small town and rural churches today if its criticisms are discussed and understood and the application of the principle is begun.

Questions For Discussion of Chapter 4

1. In your own words define the homogeneous unit principle.

2. Give some biblical validation to the homogeneous unit principle from the Old Testament. From the New Testament.

3. What are the factors that make the homogeneous unit principle effective in small town and rural churches?

4. What are your criticisms of the homogeneous unit principle?

5. List the strengths you see in the homogeneous unit principle and apply them to your church.

Footnotes

[1] Donald McGavran, *Understanding Church Growth* (Grand Rapids: William B. Eerdmans Publishing Co., 1970), p. 85.

[2] Donald McGavran, *Ethnic Realities and the Church,* (Pasadena: Wm. Carey Library, 1979), pp. 230-231.

[3] Donald McGavran, *Understanding Church Growth,* p. 183.

[4] Sweet, pp. 143-144, (source of enclosed quote not given.)

[5] Carl G. Kromminga, *Bringing God's News to Neighbors,* (Nutley, New Jersey: Presbyterian and Reformed Publishing Co., 1977) p. 16.

[6] *Ibid.,* pp. 16-17.

[7] *Ibid.,* p. 19.

[8] Michael Green, *Evangelism in the Early Church,* (Grand Rapids: Eerdmans Publishing Co., 1970), p. 26.

[9] Michael Green, p. 27.

[10] Donald A. McGavran, *Ethnic Realities and the Church,* p. 94.

[11] Donald McGavran, *Understanding Church Growth,* p. 311.

[12] *Ibid.,* p. 311.

[13] *Ibid.,* p. 312.

[14] Richard R. De Ridder, *Discipling the Nations,* (Grand Rapids: Baker Books House, 1971), p. 210-211.

[15] Harry R. Boer, *Pentecost and Missions,* (Grand Rapids: Eerdmans, 1961), p. 185.

[16] George E. Ladd, *The Gospel of the Kingdom,* (Grand Rapids: Eerdmans, 1975), p. 13.

[17] Edward R. Dayton and David A. Fraser, *Planning Strategies for World Evangelism,* (Grand Rapids: Eerdmans, 1980), p. 180.

[18] Peter Wagner, *Our Kind of People,* (Atlanta: John Knox Press, 1979), pp. 32-33, quoting McGavran, *Understanding Church Growth,* p. 198.

[19] Donald McGavran, *Understanding Church Growth,* p. 310.

[20] Donald A. McGavran, *Ethnic Realities and the Church,* p. 3.

[21] *Ibid.,* p. 3-4.

[22] Wilbert R. Shenk, *The Challenge of Church Growth — A Symposium* (Scottsdale, Pa: Herald Press, 1973), John Yoder — Chapter 2, *Church Growth Issues in Theological Perspective,* pp. 45-46.

[23] Arthur Glasser, *et. al., Crucial Dimensions in World Evangelization,* (Pasadena: William Carey Library, 1976), p. 24.

[24] *Ibid.,* p. 40.

Chapter 5

Applying the Principles of Celebration, Congregation and Cell to Small Town and Rural Churches

The principle of celebration, congregation and cell as applied to the small town and rural church is critically important to its growth. Small town and rural churches highly value all three: celebration, congregation, and cell. In order to understand the function of this principle let us first look at the importance of the act of celebration to the church. Then we will turn to the impact of celebration to the church. Then we will turn to the impact of celebration on the church; next, we'll examine the impact of various congregations on the church; and, finally, we'll consider the emphasis of the cell in the church.

The Importance of the Act of Celebration for the Church

In the small town and rural church the act of celebration is of primary importance for the congregation. Every week the members look forward with much anticipation to the act of worship and the time of being together in praise of the Lord. Rural and small town churches are serious about their worship service. Though their worship may be less pretentious than that of their city and suburban brothers and sisters, their lack of sophistication does not lessen their desire and intensity for and in worship.

The definition of the experience which Church Growth leaders call celebration is best explained by C. Peter Wagner. A person can worship God beside his bed, in the privacy of her car or in a crowded room, but the definition of the experience called celebration includes more than all of these.

The occasion for that in most churches is on Sunday morning. When a lot of people come together, hungry to meet God, a special kind of worship experience can occur. That experience is what I want to call "celebration."[1]

The history of God's people makes clear that celebrating in worship is common.

By divine appointment not only was there a weekly Sabbath, but great yearly festivals such as the Passover, Pentecost, Day of Atonement, the Feast of the Tabernacles, and later Purim and others. Something good happened to God's people during those celebrations that would not have happened without them.[2]

In the New Testament times numerous records are written of the celebration periods of the Christians. In more recent times numerous celebrations of the church-at-large have been realized as well as revivals, evangelistic campaigns and conferences within the local churches. The ideal is to plan for each Sunday as a very special time for God and his people to meet together. When the planning and praying are coordinated in the right manner, the people and God meet with tremendous results.

Some Sunday morning worship services in our churches are fun, too. Unfortunately, however, in a large number of our churches, the Sunday morning service is more like a funeral than a festival. There is nothing unauthentic about that kind of worship service — true, committed Christians can and do get through to God under such circumstances. But it is not the kind of experience that they are very enthusiastic in inviting their unconverted friends to. Why not admit it? It's no fun![3]

The excitement or lack of excitement in a worship service is important to Church Growth. When a church really learns to celebrate in worship, it has great potential to bring in new people for Christ. The new people present in worship excite the regular members. The combination of those old and new excite and ignite the church for growth.

When no excitement and/or fun in worship is experienced, the service becomes dull and unattractive.

This is probably one reason why many churches have remained small over the years. Most of them, especially when a new pastor has arrived, have tried to beef up their worship from time to time so it would be more attractive to outsiders. But in many cases nothing seems to work. The problem could very well be that the churches are simply too small. Good celebrations need lots of people to make them fun and attractive.[4]

I concur with Dr. Wagner's contention that many people make celebration fun and attractive is correct. The larger small town and rural church (two hundred worshipers or more) makes the excitement for celebation that much more electric. However, the real key to excitement in celebration for most of our small town and rural churches is capacity of the sanctuary. A church that seats fifty and only has fifteen present for celebration is going to have trouble building excitement for celebration. However, if fifty-five people show up to celebrate in that fifty-seat sanctuary, they have an overflowing crowd and the excitement grows. On the other hand if a church that seats four hundred only has fifty in attendance, then its excitement level is dampened tremendously.

We have many rural churches with small sanctuaries and adjoining rooms and small balconies. When these churches overflow into the adjoining rooms and small balconies, the regular members become excited. I have preached in scores of country sanctuaries. When they are crowded, there is electricity and excitement. Those overflowing services I have experienced have been celebrations I will never forget.

I am not trying to say here that crowds are the only way to make celebration work, but the crowd size in relationship to the sanctuary size is important to celebration.

Another important aspect of celebration is the use of music. Some small town churches have large enough attendance to recruit a decent choir with the appropriate accompaniments. These larger small town churches can use the musical gifts of the members to great advantage in celebration.

Smaller town and country churches usually have great difficulty with choirs. However, I have found that the gift of music is proportionately available among the membership. Those with the gift of music need to share their gift regularly in worship. The congregation will not tire of the repeated use of these people. On the contrary the church will be blessed by their ministry.

A church I served in my student pastorate days was an example of this use of the gift of music in celebration. One family was greatly gifted and regularly we were blessed in celebration because of their willingness to serve.

Another aspect of strong celebration is the use of the gift of preaching. By no means does the big city preacher in the large church own the book on skillful, spirit-led preaching. Actually, many of our most effective "pulpiteers" are serving in small town and rural churches. We preachers need to state the gospel truths in simple but understandable terms interspersed with stories, illustrations, and personal experiences. Then celebration will happen!

When a small town and rural church utilizes the sanctuary most effectively, uses the gift of music with the guidance of the Holy Spirit and preaches the Word in terms the listeners can understand, that church will be a growing, vibrant church. If it is lacking in numbers, the small town or rural church will not continue to be so for long. The word will go out around the community and people will come to see and hear. As a result new converts will be added to the membership and the church will grow. Eventually the church will outgrow its facilities and have to add on or relocate. Celebration is important to the growth of small town or rural church, no matter what the size of that congregation.

The Impact of the Various Congregations on the Church

Just as important as the act of celebration is the impact of the various congregations on the small town and rural church.

Every growing church has a powerful celebration.

> However, a good celebration alone does not make for a healthy, growing church. The celebration will generally be there, but it will also be properly balanced with the other two major functions of a local church: congregation and cell.[5]

The main difference between congregation and celebration is that in celebration there is little personal contact. Many can celebrate together and remain impersonal with one another. This is not so with congregation.

In the congregation the anonymity is lost. If a believer misses two or three celebrations in a row, no one is the wiser. But if he misses two or three meetings of the "congregation," he is worried over, called upon, prayed for and made to understand that there are people around him that care. Deep down, everyone needs to have others know his or her name and use it. The congregation is the place where people know each other's names.[6]

In the small town and rural church the term congregation would be the same as a fellowship group or a Sunday school class. C. Peter Wagner gained this understanding of the term congregation from reading Larry Richard's book, *A New Face for the Church.* Wagner says,

He uses "congregation" in relationship to the world "cell," and I like the terminology. Lyle Schaller, who is more sociologically oriented, calls it a "fellowship circle." I like this terminology also, although Schaller's "fellowship circle" includes both of what I join Larry Richards in calling the congregation and the cell.[7]

The term congregation can be readily understood by lay people and pastors of small town and rural churches: the fellowship groups or circles are the backbone of these churches. The size of the membership and the size of average worship attendance will determine the actual number and the potential number of congregations a church has. Dr. George Hunter III categorizes churches in America by size: the smallest third, the middle third and the largest third. Dr. Hunter says,

In confirmed membership, the smallest third have one hundred or fewer members, the middle third have between one hundred and two hundred twenty-five members, and those churches with over two hundred twenty-five members constitute the largest third of all American Protestant congregations.[8]

The size of worship attendance, which I have referred to in this chapter under celebration, is also a gauge for church size. Concerning celebration attendance Dr. Hunter says,

In worship attendance, the smallest third have forty-five or fewer people on an average Sunday, the churches in the middle range have from forty-five to one hundred twenty in worship, and the "largest" churches are those with more than one hundred twenty in average worship attendance.[9]

There are other ways of breaking out the numbers, but this scheme is as good as any.

In the West Ohio Conference of the United Methodist Church, the judicatory with which I am most familiar, the majority of rural churches fall into the category of the smallest third — that is, one hundred or fewer members and forty-five or fewer in the celebration. There are, however, a few rural churches in middle third category of one hundred to two hundred twenty-five members and forty-five to one hundred twenty in celebration. Most of the small town churches in the West Ohio Conference would seem to be in the middle third of one hundred to two hundred twenty-five members and forty-five to one hundred twenty in celebration. It would seem that a strong minority of small town churches are in the largest church category with over two hundred twenty-five members and over one hundred twenty in the celebration. I would presume that all conferences or judicatories of other denominations would have similar small town and rural churches.

In order to consider the impact of the various congregations on the small town and rural church we must understand the major characteristic of the congregation. This major characteristic is the same for congregation whether it is in a small third, middle third or larger size church.

The major characteristic of the congregation, as I see it, is that everyone in the congregation is supposed to know everyone else. Here is where the fellowship starts, although it does not end here. In smaller churches, of course, the fellowship group and the membership group are likely to be one and the same. In a church of one hundred or two hundred members you are supposed to recognize a stranger if he wanders in on Sunday morning, and you expect to be missed if for some reason you don't attend. [10]

According to Larry Richards, a congregation's size ranges from around twenty-five to two hundred fifty people. In a rural church which is usually in the smallest church size category, there are only two and probably no more than three congregations. These are probably adult Sunday school classes or possibly a choir group or maybe the Administrative Board.

In the past five years I have held Church Growth Seminars for fifty small town and rural churches. Of those fifty small town and rural churches, thirty-two (sixty-four percent) of them belonged to the smallest third of church sizes in American Protestantism. Of those thirty-two churches, twenty were rural and twelve small town. In my research, examining these smallest-third sized churches, I found the adult Sunday school class was the congregation in the church that was most influential in the church's decision-making processes. In each of these churches I found this adult class was both the main decision-making group and the main fellowship group of the church. Thus the opinion and policy setters of the church were found in the adult Sunday school class. Because the worship or celebration attendance of these churches is so small and they are so closely knit, they have difficulty in forming new growth congregations. This closeness prevents them from branching off to form other congregations within the church and from growing the church.

I served three rural churches while student pastoring several years ago and these three churches were like the twenty-five just mentioned. All thirty-two churches and my three student pastor churches were predominantly led by one family. The family orientation is good because that emphasis is needed so badly as a model for American society. However, allowing one family to run a church can sometimes be a problem. Usually one or two sets of families run the churches. This arrangement might include a committed older father and his younger brothers and brothers-in-law and his sons and nephews. One other family of the church might be intermarried with this man or one of his brothers.

Because of the close knit relationships of these leaders, the congregation is strong. Associations are not just on Sundays, but farming and other business ventures are shared throughout the week. A real caring exists among the congregation. The problem occurs when an outsider is brought into the congregation. The outsider is never really "in" because he is not "family." Even some who have joined these extended family congregations, by marriage to a family member, have felt excluded.

If the rural church is going to become a vital growing church, it will have to come to terms with this clannish or fellowship problem and learn how to overcome it. The best way for a rural congregation to overcome clannishness is to open their close knit family to outsiders completely. Outsiders can be made part of the group best when they are of the same homogeneous unit. All of the churches to which I have referred are rural, farming-oriented churches. The ones which have been growing since involvement in the Church Growth Seminars I held are the ones which are bringing into the congregations people of the rural community who have common interests. There is a clear relationship between the congregation and the homogeneous unit principle.

Congregations are homogeneous units within the larger homogeneous unit called the church or, in Church Growth terms, the celebration. Of the fifty churches I have studied, eleven (twenty-two percent) were the middle size of American churches. Of these middle-sized churches, with one hundred to two hundred twenty-five members and forty-five to one hundred twenty in celebration, ten are in small towns and one in a rural setting. These churches have more potential for growth because they have more than one congregation already. They will grow, and some already are, if they use these fellowship groups as evangelistic tools for the gospel. These churches still experience the strong influence of a few families but more families are involved and the leadership is spread among several families. As these groups or congregations reach out, they can evangelize their neighbors who are unchurched through bringing them into their homogeneous congregational unit.

The last seven churches I have studied are in the larger church category. They consist of fourteen percent of the total churches I have studied and four are in small towns and three in rural areas (all fifty of these churches are in the American Midwest). All seven of these churches have several congregations at work recruiting new converts for the gospel within the congregations. All seven are growing churches because they understand this principle of celebration, congregation, and cell as vital to the church's growth.

One of the churches has over 1,000 members and averages over three hundred fifty for worship. The choir and music program of the church constitutes a congregation of the church. This congregation made a tour a few years ago using their musical gifts to assist churches in Europe. They also have several active Sunday school classes and groups.

Another of the churches is in a rural setting and, with a membership of about three hundred, averages over two hundred in worship. This church also has several adult classes and caters particularly to young families.

A third church of the larger church category is the church where I served previously for over twelve years as pastor. We believed so strongly in the development of congregations that we added four new adult classes in four years. These new congregations were the fellowship circles or congregations that brought many new members into the front doors of membership and have kept them in the church. Eighty percent of the net gain of the one hundred new members who joined in the last seven years I pastored there did not go out the back door because they had been joined lovingly into one of the many congregations. The average attendance in 1973 was one hundred forty-five and in 1984 — two hundred eighteen. Our Sunday school had grown in the same period from sixty-seven to one hundred thirty-two. We owed this growth partially to the strength of our congregations.

In concluding this section on the impact of the various congregations on the church it must be emphasized that these fellowship groups are essential for making churches grow. People need to feel wanted and these groups fulfill that need.

> *Church leaders make the point that the growing congregation has groups in various stages of constant formation and dissolution. Further, these groups are visually at some distance from the watchful eye of the official board, since they are forming and disbanding upon the initiative of leadership from within and are only loosely connected with the authority structures of the church.*[11]

Emphasis on the Cell in the Church

Probably more has been written by church leaders in recent years on the emphasis of the cell in the church than on celebration and congregation combined. The interest in the cell life in a church is very high. The small town and rural church understands the experience found in cell groups probably more than all other types of churches. Each church with which I have been involved as pastor or as Church Growth consultant has had effective cells at work.

> *The cell, sometimes called a "small group" is a very special relationship. It is so close to a family situation that I like to call it a "kinship circle" to contrast it from the membership circle and the fellowship circle.*[12]

The revival of the concept of cell is especially relevent to the small town and rural church today since its foundations were in small group and Sunday school class.

Even though most of us do not like to bare our souls to others, the commitment we find in doing so is helpful to our relationship to God and others. A cell or small group helps our relationship to God and it strengthens our relationships with others through our help from and intimate associations with the small group.

C. Peter Wagner told us, in the midst of Church Growth courses, that he was not a small group person, but he realized that small groups made him a better person. His pastor once told him, "You're a fine Christian, but you'll be a much better one if you let God get ahold of you in a small group."

> *I also listen to people like Larry Richards who have a deep personal involvement in spreading the small group movement through churches in America. Here is how he defines the cell: "Eight or twelve believers gathered to minister to each other, to grow in their sensed love and unity, and to encourage one another to full commitment to Christ."*[13]

To those of us who have studied Wesley, this definition of a cell sounds hauntingly familiar.

One-hundred percent of those people who were involved in cells in the ministries I have had, were solid committed Christians. The cells of the small town and rural churches I have studied report the same results. The ideal, therefore, is to involve everyone who comes to know Christ and joins the church in a cell. I have not been able to reach that ideal. The cell is, however, the spiritual backbone and strength of the small town and rural church.

Let's conclude. The principle of celebration, congregation and cell, as applied to small town and rural churches, is crucial for growth in those churches. C. Peter Wagner concludes that this principle applied to a church will, along with other major Church Growth functions, bring growth.

Remember: Celebration + Congregation + Cell = Church[14]

The next chapter will discuss the Church Growth principle of *redemption and lift* as applied to the small town and rural church. The discussion will include the emphasis of redemption as unqualified good and the dangers of lift as a qualified good.

Questions for Discussion of Chapter 5

1. What is the importance of celebration for the life of your church?

2. How can your church improve its celebration?

3. How does your congregation relate to the homogeneous unit principle?

4. How many congregations are in your church? List them and identify your strengths and weaknesses.

5. List ways you can involve new members in cell groups in your church.

Footnotes

[1]C. Peter Wagner, *Your Church Can Grow,* p. 97.

[2]*Ibid.,* p. 98.

[3]*Ibid.,* p. 98.

[4]*Ibid.,* p. 98-99.

[5]*Ibid.,* p. 100.

[6]*Ibid.,* p. 101.

[7]*Ibid.,* p. 101.

[8]George Hunter III, *Church Growth Strategies That Work,* p. 83.

[9]*Ibid.,* p. 83.

[10]C. Peter Wagner, *Your Church Can Grow,* pp. 101-102.

[11]Carl S. Dudley, *Making the Small Church Effective* (Abingdon: Nashville, 1979), p. 154.

[12]C. Peter Wagner, *Your Church Can Grow,* p. 107.

[13]*Ibid.,* p. 108.

[14]*Ibid.,* p. 109.

Chapter 6

Applying the Principles of Redemption and Lift to Small Town and Rural Churches

The principle of redemption and lift has been a part of the Christian church since its beginning in the first century. Basically redemption and lift means that when a person or group of persons accept Christ as Savior those social and economic positions which they occupied prior to conversion become unacceptable to them. This resulting dissatisfaction leads this person or these individuals to want to change their social and economic conditions. This phenomena is called lift. This principle of redemption and lift needs to be examined and understood as it is applied to the small town and rural churches.

Redemption as Unqualified Good

The grass roots of conservatism and orthodoxy within most denominations are found in their rural and small town churches. Within these churches the emphasis upon redemption is essential to their existence. The foundation of the rural and small town churches is a solid grounding in the change that Jesus Christ can make on an individual or a group of individuals' lives. These churches were started ten, fifty or two-hundred years ago with the desire to win individuals to Jesus Christ.

In his discussion of the act of redemption Donald McGavran says,

Every true Church observes among its members a redemption due to Christ's saving activity in the human heart. When Christ comes in, man becomes a new creation. He repents and turns from his sins.

He gains victory over pride, greed, laziness, drink, hate, and envy.
He ceases quarreling with his neighbors and chasing women. He turns
from litigation to constructive activity. He educates his children. He
learns what God requires of him, and worships regularly. He be-
comes a more effective human being. [1]

Dr. McGavran's statement on true redemption sounds very evangelical in its scope. The membership vows one takes when he or she
joins the church are based on the very essence of McGavran's
statement.

In the rural and small town church the importance of redemption is usually not downplayed. Fellow believers rejoice at the adding
of one new fellow believer to the kingdom of God. The emphasis
on Bible study and prayer groups is strong. Of the fifty rural and
small town churches in which I have held Church Growth Seminars,
the importance of redemption as bedrock to the gospel message is
unquestioned. Only one individual in all the seminars I have conducted has questioned me when we discussed the primary importance
of fulfilling the Great Commission (Matthew 28) of preaching the
gospel to all people so that none are externally lost. Rural and small
town lay persons who lead their churches are convinced of the lost-
ness of humanity unless humanity finds Christ.

In the small town and rural church the emphasis upon redemption is a pure emphasis. Redemption is an unqualified good.

Redemption, depending solely on the Bible, the Church, the Savior,
the Holy Spirit, and prayer, is indefinitely reproducible. Wherever
men trust Christ, read His Word, obey Him, and gather round His
table they are redeemed in this way, even when wholly independent
of any aid from abroad. [2]

This redemption is unqualified in its good for the local church, for
the individuals in the church and most importantly for the life of
the individual who has been saved.

The rural and small town church that makes this biblical emphasis
upon salvation is usually a growing church. In areas of decreasing
population, the small town and rural churches can survive if they
are properly motivated to the kind of aggressive evangelism that the
New Testament advocates.

> *The picture of declining population in rural areas does not necessarily mean stagnation. Some of the most stable Christians in American society live in the rural areas. Survival in agriculture requires wise planning and sound financing. Many Christians in rural areas have giving power which cannot yet be matched by their urban brothers.*
>
> *Rural congregations are often thriving today in spite of declining populations in rural areas. The automobile (frequently two or three per family) has made transportation a minor item. Rural families may drive twenty miles or more to participate in an active church. A congregation with a house of worship in the open country can draw worshipers from surrounding towns and villages if it has an aggressive evangelistic program. Denominational barriers are becoming less and less important to Americans. They will worship where they are wanted and where the Bible is still being preached and taught.*[3]

Since redemption is an unqualified good, the emphasis of the church must be geared to evangelism of the lost. The small town and rural church needs to keep that emphasis as its foundation. Small town and rural lay leadership needs to be strong in its redemptive emphasis.

When I went to the Convoy, Ohio, United Methodist Church, the church was declining in attendance at both church and Sunday church school. The lay leadership quizzed and questioned me concerning my theological emphasis and doctrinal position. When they understood that my emphasis was going to be biblically evangelistic, they immediately became optimistic about the growth potential of the church. Four "blondes" (my name for senior citizen ladies in my church whose hair has lightened in color because of age) in the church told me they had been secretly praying for several years for the Lord to send me to the church. They did not know me personally but when the church accepted my appointment they were assured in their hearts that I was the pastor for whom they had been praying.

From that beginning, filled with prayer and anticipation, our church at Convoy grew from three hundred sixty-nine members when I started in 1973 to five hundred twenty members by the end of 1984. Our worship attendance also grew (see chart on page 146). We were able to reach people who were in need of a Savior because our emphasis was on redemption as an unqualified good. Many other small town and rural churches can tell the same story. However, the sad story is that these growing small town and rural churches which are not growing *can* grow if they once again emphasize the importance of redemption and once again begin an evangelistic campaign that is deliberate and biblical. The results will obviously be a revitalized and growing small town and rural church. The results will also include a pleasantly surprised bishop or other judicatory leader. The results will be a growing, vital small town or rural church that had put an emphasis on redemption as an unqualified good.

The Dangers of Lift as a Qualified Good

In his studies of mission churches around the world Dr. Donald McGavran discovered the phenomenon of lift although it has been apparent in Christianity since its beginnings.

In discussing the phenomenon of lift McGavran says,

> *A second kind of improvement, which I am calling "lift," is due to church and mission activities. The congregation and its members have the great benefit of medicine, education, loving friendship, and protection. the founding mission or Church establishes schools, hospitals, agricultural centers, literary classes, and many other institutions to serve and help the general public and specially the new brothers in Christ. If these are illiterate, they are taught to read. Their children, attending church and mission schools — or, increasingly, tax-supported schools — become grade-school, high-school, and college graduates. Perhaps they go to Christian vocational schools to become mechanics, radio technicians, or artisans. Girls, sent to nurses' or teachers' training schools, are snapped up by the rapidly expanding government health and education programs and get good salaries.* [4]

These people and their children improve their social and economic standing. They also improve the standards of their communities. If they were lower-class people, they immediately improve themselves and soon become middle-class. The whole community of believers shares in newfound personal self-worth and gratification. In conclusion Dr. McGavran says "All this I am calling 'lift.' " [5]

Lift can be a great asset to the growth and maturation of the church. But some dangers can occur which need to be examined and understood. An example of lift being a danger in the church I served at Convoy, Ohio, is illustrated in the story of a person I will call John.

John was from a lower socio-economic class and lived in our town for several years prior to his conversion. He had moved to our community from another state; this made him an outsider. John was into the drug scene and also dependent on alcohol. One night he came to my home in a drunken stupor, yet equally high on drugs, and wanted to make a profession for Christ. I could hardly understand his speech, yet somehow through the Holy Spirit, he was able to express to me what he wanted. The next evening a completely transformed individual from head to foot came to my door. John had gone home, slept off his addiction, showered, shaved, had a haircut and put on some decent clothes. He was polite — and apologetic about his appearance and manners the previous night. John was genuinely saved and his appearance was a witness to his transformation.

From that day on John became a part of our church and brought his family to our services and functions. His wife was a backslidden member of another denomination. She immediately rejoiced in his conversion and recommitted her life to Christ.

John began improving his personal situation immediately. He began fixing his home, one that was badly in need of repair. Not only did he buy a new car, one that was comparable to the ones the members of the church drove, but he purchased new furniture over the next several months as well. He was a common laborer and he wanted to improve his work status. With the help of some concerned men of the church he received some managerial training and became a foreman in a local business.

John's leadership abilities were evident, and within a year he helped me implement a calling program for the church, a program of which he became the founding chairman. John was happy in his newfound life and experience. He loved his brothers in Christ with whom he worked in the church. He was happy and he evidently had experienced lift after his genuine conversion.

All went well for about two years, until John realized his wife was not happy. Over a period of months of counseling, I discovered her unhappiness. She was not happy with the new furniture, the new car, the new physical appearance of John. She was glad he was saved, but she saw no need for all the social changes. She did not feel at ease with the wives of John's friends in our church. They were different from her and she had no intention of being lifted to their social class. She was happy remaining a Christian in the social class where she had been previously.

Subsequently John and his wife had to work through their now-vastly-different ways of thinking. As a result they had to move away from our community and live in another area where John's wife felt at home. The experience was a painful one for our church to be involved in and caused much sadness. From this experience we learned that lift has its dangers.

There are no dangers in the experience of redemption. To all who are redeemed immediate victory over sin and its resulting selfishness can be realized. To those who are redeemed there is the promise of the ultimate victory which is in Christ Jesus. That ultimate victory is an unmerited share of the eternal victory. Donald McGavran is right when he claims for redemption unqualified good.

This unqualified good does not exist with lift. Following redemption comes the climbing to higher social or economic heights. Donald McGavran is again right to claim for lift qualified good. What then are the dangers of lift as a qualified good?

One danger of lift in the small town and rural church is the fact that, once a person is redeemed, he or she begins losing contact with his or her former friends. The resulting problem is that his or her lift to the new life and life-style separates him or her from his or her old friends and their life-style. The best way to overcome this danger is for him or her, immediately upon his or her conversion, to introduce his or her old friends to those who are qualified to evangelize. The evangelists can determine from the new convert's friends which ones are receptive. This method has been called the web concept. The idea is to explore and exploit as many of the new converts' social networks as possible while he or she is still relatively close to them. Also, immediate involvement of the new convert in a congregation of the church (such as a Sunday school class) is important.

The fact that a great majority of people come to Christ and the local church through webs of relationships has great implications for your Sunday school and your church.[6]

The danger of lift can be alleviated by applying the Church Growth principle of webs.

There are groups of people who can be reached in small town and rural communities by winning one of them and through that one's conversion winning his whole social network of contacts. One small town or rural church could grow by several new members over a relatively short period of time by using this method.

One danger of lift, then, is that goodness and educational advancement from lift separates the redeemed from his or her former web network. The example of John, previously cited, shows how goodness and education separated John from his own family. Ultimately John had to move away and find other work in order to save his marriage and his family relationships because our church was a different homogeneous unit than that which his wife was comfortable. He lifted himself to the level of our homogeneous unit by education; yet his wife lagged behind. Thus, strain came to their marriage because of lift.

The lift that causes educational advancement and separation is hard to stop. The church must be aware of this danger and be ready to help the individual cope with the problem.

Another danger in lift is what we might call "holier than thou" syndrome. When a person lifts himself or herself to a new experience, looks back and feels superior to his or her former social network, his or her attitude may be dangerous. Small town and rural church have this problem. We who have been saved sometimes communicate an attitude of spiritual arrogance to our former friends in the community. Since the community is small and we run into one another regularly through the course of a week, the tension between former friends grows because of the frequent contacts. Those outside the faith — former friends — tend to call us hypocritical. They ask themselves why we feel we are better than they are. This kind of separation will halt the growth of the church immediately. We need to keep the channels of love open between us and the people outside. Much work is involved in a church maintaining contacts with those outside the church without cultivating "holier than thou" syndrome. Much difficulty is encountered in rural and small town settings because of the frequent intermingling from social contacts.

An additional danger in lift is that lift in many small town and rural churches is a protective mechanism against sin. By this I mean that many small town and rural churches are so separated from "the world" and worldliness that they tend to draw a new convert very rapidly away from the world. Then the new convert and his or her new friends have no contact with his or her former associates. An example would be that of a wayward son. Once that son is plucked from the sinful life and returned to the Christian nest, he is so safely kept that there is no hope for reaching his lost generation of friends. We deprogram him immediately and rush him through the stages of lift in order to keep him saved from his former life. Donald McGavran says,

> When lift is so rapid that it breaks social contact between Christians and their non-Christian relatives, it ceases to be an unqualified good. Change of language, style of living, clothing, and occupation may appear desirable. These Christians are making great progress, churchmen say. But if these same changes tear the Christians away from their communities, they are dubious blessings.[7]

While we are afraid of sin, we need to trust in the power of God to use the changed life of the new convert as a glorious witness to the old acquaintances in order to win them. The danger can be overcome by trusting in the power of God to use us as his witnesses to win others. After all, we are saved, ultimately, to tell others, not for self-isolation.

"Some might object to this whole argument, which subordinates lift to redemption, on the grounds that the church must lift people up."[8] There is no doubt that lift is important to redemption. We need to proclaim the better life, the lifted state above the sinful nature. The purpose of this discussion is not to dilute the riches of Christ offered in salvation. The real purpose is, instead, to warn leaders in rural and small town churches that there are dangers unique to our communities and churches because we are small town and rural. The final note is that these dangers can successfully be overcome or alleviated.

In the chapter to come we will discuss the understanding of resistance and receptivity in rural and small town communities. We will identify who the resistant are in rural and small town comunities and who the receptive are in those communities.

Questions for Discussion of Chapter 6

1. Why is redemption unqualified good?

2. What does the fact of lift being a qualified good mean to you and your church?

3. What are some dangers of lift which you have seen in the church?

4. How important is redemption and lift to the small town and rural church?

[1]Donald McGavran, *Understanding Church Growth,* p. 261.

[2]*Ibid.,* p. 261.

[3]Paul Benjamin, *The Growing Congregation,* (Lincoln, Ill.: Lincoln Christian College Press, 1972), p. 45.

[4]Donald McGavran, *Understanding Church Growth,* pp. 261, 262.

[5]*Ibid.,* p. 262.

[6]Charles Arn, *Growth: A New Vision For The Sunday School,* p. 80.

[7]Donald McGavran, *Understanding Church Growth,* p. 270.

[8]*Ibid.,* p. 275.

Chapter 7

Understanding Resistance and Receptivity in Rural and Small Town Communities

Who are the resistant and who are the receptive? That question is one I have been asking myself for the past ten years since I have been involved in the Church Growth movement. Prior to ten years ago my whole emphasis as a United Methodist minister was to reach the whole community where I served because I was taught in seminary to reach everybody for Christ. After all, my professors had reminded me, "The world was my parish," as the founder of Methodism, John Wesley had said. My "world" was to be the community where I was serving. It was my commitment to the Lord to give my best to win to the Lord everyone I could in that community.

Then I heard George Hunter and Peter Wagner talk about the homogeneous unit principle and the principle of resistance and receptivity. Having those Church Growth principles defined for me, I began to see my mandate to evangelize from a much different perspective. This new perspective was a real revelation to me since I had never understood my total calling into the ministry before that time. But the definition of these Church Growth principles opened my understanding. I was now able to see the calling I had received in a different way.

Before I define these principles, let me tell you my story. As a ten-year-old boy, I experienced a definite call to preach. At that time God spoke to me concerning my call to preach. God revealed to me that he wanted me to be an evangelist. I knew, therefore, that my preaching would be evangelistic in nature. The resulting many years of preparation, and the unfolding of my call, revealed to me that

God had given me as a primary gift the gift of evangelism. This gift in turn coincided with my calling to be an evangelist. As I began my ministry, I was evangelistic in nature. Having discovered my gift, I had developed it. God used that gift to win many lost through me.

However, many times I found myself evangelizing a congregation which had already been evangelized. What they were needing was nurture and growth so they could develp their gifts and bring the lost in for evangelizing.

Another misunderstanding of evangelizing I had came to light in my relationships with people I personally enjoyed. Because I enjoyed being with them, I called on them regularly and witnessed to them often, but no soul-winning took place. I would become discouraged. Still, because I enjoyed their company, I would return to them, only to spend more fruitless time. This led to more frustration on my part. If I would have understood then that I was experiencing resistance from that person or family, I would have saved both of us a great deal of time.

Other times I went into communities, or to groups of people within the community, only to find them resistant to me and my church but receptive to another pastor and church. I did not understand the homogeneous unit principle, that those people were resistant because we were of different homogeneous units.

On the other side of resistance is receptivity. On many occasions I missed a great opportunity to share the gospel with a person when that person was wide open. As I look back now, I see that I was too busy to go to a church meeting; or I found that person was not interesting to talk to; or there was some other excuse.

But then I began studying Church Growth — and the homogeneous unit principle and the phenomena of resistance and receptivity. Now my emphasis has completely changed. "The world is still my parish," as John Wesley said, yet I see within my world the parish that God sends to me. Some of them are resistant to my church and our evangelistic pleas. Yet some who are resistant today through circumstances or a crisis can become receptive tomorrow. Consequently, these resistant are part of my parish; I love them and keep contact with them until they are ready, but I really spend my time with those who are open to gospel.

The other group which is part of my parish is made up of the receptive ones. They are ready and willing to make a commitment to Christ. I am excited about ministering to them and our church is excited about seeing their new-found awareness of God and his goodness. These new converts become new converts because they are receptive, and we take advantage of their receptivity. Our church is blessed and we all grow together.

I have found my experiences with those who are resistant and receptive vital to the understanding of my calling to preach, a calling I received as a ten-year-old boy. Even my earlier awareness of my gift for evangelism, and the subsequent nurturing of that gift, was not enough. I had also to understand and begin applying the principle of resistance and receptivity.

In rural and small town America the walls of resistance and receptivity are pronounced. A rural and small town community is a highly personal community because everyone knows everyone else's business. Thus, a high level of tolerance to different viewpoints and levels of understanding exists. Those who plan to evangelize a rural or a small town community must understand inner workings of rural and small town communities. From my experiences in pastoring both small town and rural churches I am now better able to know whom to contact and whom to evangelize. I know this because I now understand the phenomena of receptivity and resistance.

What are the problems and opportunities of a small town and rural community in terms of its resistance to the gospel or its receptivity to the gospel? Let's begin by defining these two Church Growth terms.

The founder of the Church Growth movement, Dr. Donald McGavran, initiated the receptivity/resistance principle. A receptive person is one who is willing to hear the message of the gospel because of some event, happening or experience in his or her life. This event, happening or experience can be of a negative, traumatic nature, or it can be of a positive nature. On the other hand, a resistant person is a person who has built walls around himself or herself against the message of the gospel. This person is not interested in hearing the gospel message in any way, shape or form. It must always be remembered by those of us who are involved in the work of evangelism that a resistant person today can become a receptive person tomorrow. The reverse is also true; a receptive person tonight can become a resistant person by tomorrow morning.

Our Lord spoke of fields in which the seed had just been sown and those ripe to harvest. Sometimes men hearing the Word do nothing.

The field appears no nearer harvest after receiving the seed than it did before. Sometimes, however, men hearing the word leap to obey it. They receive it with joy, go down into the waters of baptism, and come up to Spirit-filled lives in self-propagating congregations. [1]

The ups-and-downs of people's temperature — warmth or coldness towards the gospel — is a worldwide and age-old phenomenon. Every evangelist and missionary needs to study people and their responses, both positive and negative, toward the gospel.

Our Lord took account of the varying ability of individuals and societies to hear and obey the Gospel. Fluctuating receptivity is the most prominent aspect of human nature and society. It marks the urban and the rural, advanced and primitive, educated and illiterate. [2]

There seems to be an unevenness of growth among people and groups of people toward the gospel.

Peoples and societies also vary in responsiveness. Whole segments of mankind resist the Gospel for periods — often very long periods — and then ripen to the Good News. In resistant populations single congregations only, and those small, can be created and kept alive, whereas in responsive ones many congregations which freely reproduce others can be established. [3]

Who Are the Resistant Peoples in the Rural and Small Town Church Setting?

Who are the resistant peoples in rural and small town communities? Whoever they are, we need always to remember that they are not to be forgotten. Dr. McGavran says,

Recognition of variations in receptivity is resisted by some mission thinkers because they fear that, if they accept it, they will be forced to abandon resistant fields. Abandonment is not called for. Fields must be sown. Stony fields must be plowed before they are sown. No one should conclude that if receptivity is low, the Church should withdraw mission. [4]

Therefore, Dr. McGavran suggests the evangelistic thrust be light in unreceptive or resistant fields.

110

*They will turn receptive some day. They also have children of God
living in them. Their populations are made up of men and women
of whom Christ died. While they continue in their rebellious and
resistant state, they should be given the opportunity to hear the
Gospel in as courteous a way as possible. But they should not be
heavily occupied lest, fearing that they will be swamped by Christians, they become even more resistant.*[5]

Who are the resistant peoples in rural and small town communities? Let us look first at resistant rural people, and then the small
town resistant.

Resistant Rural People

Resistant rural people are the smallest group in America. They
have few reasons to be resistant. However, since there *are* resistant
rural people, we need to study their reasons for resistance and how
they might be overcome.

One type of resistant rural people is the bad luck or bitter. They
have not been like Job and turned to God for help in their tragedy.
These people have had much "bad luck," as people of the world
call it. In their opinion, life has dealt them a bitter blow. They have
lost their property through a storm and their insurance policy ran
out just a week before that storm. Their crops have failed two years
in a row. Their children have all turned against them. When one
even mentions the Lord to them. they quickly turn that suggestion
aside. These bitter people are extremely difficult to reach because
they are angry at God and reject him for help because they feel he
has rejected them. To convince them otherwise is almost impossible.

Another resistant rural type is the self-sufficient. This individual
has as his or her philosophy of life, "I can do it." This person has
not had much trouble in life and has been able to take care of his
or her family. This person is usually well off financially, perhaps
a rich landowner, and money buys whatever he seems to need. If
one of his family becomes sick, he takes that one to the best hospi-
tal where the best medical doctors are available. Money is no object. He feels confident with himself and is self-sufficient in all areas
of his life. John Wesley encountered the resistance of these landowners. He was known to resist rich farmers and landowners because he was aware they were resistant to the gospel.

The Small Town Resistant

In the small towns across America there are people who are resistant to the gospel. The first group of resistant I have found, in every small town where I have served, or where I have held a Church Growth workshop, are those who have no church of their homogeneous unit. In fact, this obstacle might be the biggest resistance obstacle in the small towns. The Southern Baptists realized this problem and launched a Bold Missions Thrust to the Midwest to win these seemingly unwinnable people.

The problem with these resistant is that they are turned off by the established churches in their communities because they feel alienated from these churches. The homogeneous unit principle says that people like to be with people who are like themselves. Many of our small towns in America do not have churches which can reach significant portions of those small communities because the existing churches are not of the homogeneous unit of those people. They, therefore, are turned off by evangelistic efforts and are resistant to the existing organized churches. The Southern Baptists and many independent and charismatic groups have moved into small towns. They have started rapidly growing and successful ministries because they broke the resistance of these people by sending missionaries and ministers who could reach their homogeneous unit. They, in turn, have developed church services and types of ministries that have appealed to those resistant people. The result has been phenomenal. The existing United Methodist, Lutheran and other denominations have not been able to figure out why people they have found resistant for years, sometimes their neighbors, have suddenly become receptive to a whole new group of people and ministry. The reason is evident to those of us in the Church Growth movement. These resistants were resistant to the existing church people because they were of a different homogeneous unit.

Another resistant group in the small towns are the bitter, who are similar to the bitter of the rural setting. Their excuses and rejection of the gospel are rooted in the same reasons as the rural, bitter people.

Another resistant group in the small towns of America are the social and civic-minded. These people, who are out to help the community, are ready to serve when called upon and are active in community affairs. Usually belonging to one or more civic and social organizations, they will work hard for the community and are involved heavily when the community is in crisis. Most of them come from Christian families and went to church in their youth.

I have found these social and civic-minded resistant people in every small town I have studied. For a support group in time of need they depend upon one another. At the time of death in one of the families, these friends will take off work and spend literally hours with these families. They will, through their civic and social organizations, put on a funeral dinner for a family with no strings attached.

I came to know about this resistant group because I was the "pastor" of over three hundred of them in my previous church community. They called upon me to minister to them when a crisis or death occurred in their family. Then they allowed me to minister to them and share with them the gospel. However, they did not need the church where I pastored because they had a large network of friends who comforted them. When the crisis was over, they were back to life as usual and I could not minister to them again until the next crisis. One reason for their resistance was that they were not of my church's homogeneous unit and did not feel at home in our church. They felt at home with *me* but not the *church*. Since no other churches in our community were reaching their homogeneous unit, they could not be evangelized. Another reason they rejected the church was that they felt good about helping others individually and through community organizations. They were working their way for salvation by doing good works. Thus they did not feel the need for the church.

One way to reach these social and civic-minded resistant people would be to start a church of their group or homogeneous unit. The Southern Baptists, independents and charismatics have been doing just that and are having great success. These churches are reaching this group, as they are reaching the group with no homogeneous unit.

I have noticed that there is one item common to all of this group. Their commonality is an enjoyment of, and leisure pastime with, alcohol consumption. In other words, they enjoy drinking together and feel uncomfortable around Christians who only drink alcohol occasionally or not at all. I have found alcohol to be an important social mixer (pun intended) for this group. One must understand the importance of alcohol to these people in order possibly to reach them.

Another resistant group in the small towns are the single, divorced parents and mixed families of those remarried because of divorce.

In the city the church is dealing with this new breed of single, divorced, one-parent family and remarried divorced. Many of our large denominational churches have developed ministries for these groups of people, but the small town, with its strong family ties and orientation, excludes the divorced and remarried because of divorce. The small town church is conservative in its thinking toward divorce. Because of its strong family orientation, the small town church is unable to relate theologically to this group. Therefore, the group suffers because it feels alienated to the church and thus is resistant to the gospel.

In the small town we find the resistant. We find individuals who are resistant because there is no group of their homogeneous unit. We also find the resistant because of bitterness. Another resistant group is the social and civic-minded. The last resistant group is the single, divorced parents and those who remarry after divorce. These are some of the most predominant resistant groups found in small town communities.

We need to stress, however, that those resistant today might be responsive tomorrow. These resistant lead us to our next section: those who are the receptive people in rural and small town communities. It is interesting to note the similarities between of the resistant and the receptive.

The Understanding of Receptive Peoples in Rural and Small Town Churches

The word "receptive" is key to the work of evangelism, and has been since the early first century church. The word "receptive" is essential to the understanding and implementation of Church Growth. The Apostle Paul went into the towns and villages looking for receptive people. He found a large, receptive audience among the Greeks who were already responsive to the Jewish religion. Paul started and developed great churches among these people. Our goal in finding and reaching receptive people in rural and small town comunities is to bring them to conversion, find a place for them in the membership of in the local church, and make them effective disciples of Jesus Christ. These objectives — and these objectives only — are our motives. C. Peter Wagner says,

> *All church growth is not equally good growth. Although there are
> exceptions, the most beneficial kind of growth is conversion growth.
> That is what Acts 2:47 refers to. This is also called Kingdom growth
> because new members are being brought into the Kingdom of God.*[6]

It is essential that we agree upon the motivation for seeking receptive people. It is, the gospel mandate to seek and win the lost. God
leads us to the lost among the peoples of the world. We concentrate
our efforts among those of the lost who are receptive to the gospel
message.

Receptive People in Rural Areas

Who are the receptive people in rural areas? The first group is
those who want Christian teaching for their families. According to
research conducted by the Institute for American Church Growth
in Pasadena, California, there are eight categories of people who
were once receptive and are now active members of their church.
They came to membership through:

Special Need	2%
Walk-In	3%
Pastor	6%
Visitation	1%
Sunday School	5%
Evangelistic Crusades	½ of 1%
Program	3%
Friend/Relative	79%

All of these categories are important because they are used to
bring receptive people into the church.

> *Does this enormous percentage of people who come into the church
> because of a friend or relative (and the comparatively small percen-
> tage that come into the church as a result of the Sunday School)
> mean that the Sunday School should be downplayed as an outreach
> priority? Not at all. The fact is that a majority of people presently
> in church came in through the Sunday School.*[8]

Hence, people in the rural area who come into the church come
because they want their children in some kind of religious education.

They also feel inadequate in *their own* understanding of Christian teaching, making it easy to reach them.

How then do these receptive people, usually young married couples with small children, come into the church?

> *The reason people first come into a new life in Chirst and the local church is through the influence of a friend or relative. The place of first contact with the church is most often the Sunday School.*[9]

We find these young, rural couples receptive to the gospel because their roots are usually in a Christian home and they want to rear their children in a Christian home. The key group to make the first evangelistic impression upon this group is usually their close friends or relatives who are Christians. The results of the Institute for American Church Growth study indicate that seventy-nine percent who join the church and become active are won initially by a close friend or relative.

The former church I served was in a small town, and we had been able to reach forty new rural, young families for Christ in just four years because we knew these families had a need for Christian education for their children. We had reached all forty, or one hundred percent of them, through friends or relatives who were already active in our church.

In Church Growth terminology this method is called the web movement.

> *Webs are social ties between people. They are immediate family ties and extended family ties. They are relationships with people at work or at school or play. They are friendship ties and common interest ties. The people most responsive to your Sunday School outreach efforts and most likely to be added to your church will be found within the webs of members presently in your Sunday School. And when a new person comes into your Sunday School, it does more than add one additional person to the roll. It opens a brand new untapped web consisting of the person's friends and family now outside the church and Sunday School. The Sunday School desiring growth is enormously interested in all such webs.*[10]

A rural church that is growing is a church that has a strong Christian education program and that is reaching young couples who want to rear their children in the Christian faith.

Another group that is receptive in rural areas are the down-and-out people. There are many old farm houses across our land and the farmers are renting these old homes cheaply. Those poor families from the city and towns are moving to these homes to get away from the poverty and drudgery of the large cities and towns. The church's local mission program can reach these people and win them to Christ. Consequently, they can be lifted after their redemption to newer and better lifestyles. They are receptive because they are down-and-out, and they are open to the claims of the gospel and the love shared by the people of the church.

Another receptive group in rural areas are people who have escaped the cities for the more tranquil rural life. These are not poor escapees; they are affluent middle class people. The city has frustrated them, so that many of them buy homes in the country and commute by car, bus or train thirty to sixty miles every day in exchange for the privilege of being away from city life. The easy-going rural church can attract these displaced persons for two reasons. First, they are in transition themselves and their movement from the city signified their transitional mood. Second, the tranquil country church is a real weekend blessing to them, a sort of retreat from the weekly grind. The rural church needs to reach these receptive escapees of the city, for they are available and more and more of them are building and buying in the country.

Be alert to these receptive people in the rural areas: those who want Christian teaching for their families, the down-and-out people and city escapees. The rural church can reach these receptive groups when it becomes aware of them and begins a strategy of evangelism to reach them.

People Who Are Receptive in Towns

Some people who are receptive in towns belong to groups which parallel the rural dwellers. One group of town receptives are those who want Christian teaching for their families. They are much like their rural counterparts and they can be reached. The small town church needs to see their need and then fill it. Robert Schuller's stated strategy is "Find a need and fill it." Another group of town receptives which parallel the rural is the city escapee group. They are receptive to the gospel and the small town church can reach this group effectively.

A third group of people who are receptive in small towns are family groupings or clans which have moved into that area from another part of the country or who have come from another religious background or who have come from another country. This group is unusual but a reality today in the small towns. In the Southwest and West these would be the Indians and Mexicans. Around Florida and other southern states are the South American boat people. In many small towns in America are the Vietnamese and Far Eastern people. In the Midwest there are more black families moving to small towns. The southerner has moved North for jobs and even most recently because of economic changes the midwesterners are flocking into small towns in Texas and other southern states.

If possible, these people move in groups and become extremely close and clannish. Their social background is different from others in the community and they feel out of place; thus they are receptive to the gospel. The church in a small town will have to work with these receptive people in a different way because they are different from the town folk. A church within the church can be started with joint services for the new group and the original congregation from time to time. With much care and planning these people can be reached by the small town church.

The last group of receptives in a small town community are what I call the "outsiders." They might have lived in the community for years, but they still feel as excluded as the city escapees and the clans that move there. Members of this group have not intermarried with popular town families, nor had a town store or residential street named after them. They have not inherited money from a rich uncle, nor won a beauty contest, nor contributed the star basketball player to the school's state championship team twenty years ago. Their lives have been uneventful and drab and they are lonely. Thus, they are receptive because they feel like outsiders. The small town church needs to recognize these people and minister to them. They have great potential for coming alive in Christ.

These small town receptives and rural receptives are potentially open for evangelism and Church Growth. The small town and rural churches in America need to bridge existing gaps in order to reach these people and win them to Christ. Even though they are receptive, one cannot conclude that they are signed, sealed and bound for Heaven. They need to be evangelized because they are potentially receptive people. If established small town and rural churches do not reach them, some other denomination might disciple them — or even non-Christian groups. Or, tragically, they will be lost forever.

Resistance and Receptivity in Rural and Small Town Communities in the First Century Church

Preparatory to effectively reaching these receptive people in small town and rural communities in America and further develop a strategy to win them for Christ, it is well to look at the Scriptures for guidance. How did resistance and receptivity surface in rural and small town communities in the church in the first century?

The Apostle Paul was a bondservant of Christ Jesus. The definition of *bondservant* is "slave." The Apostle Paul was a slave of and for Jesus Christ. His commitment as a slave for Jesus Christ is seen in 1 Corinthians 9:19-22.

This passage reminds us Paul was willing to become "all things to all men." The result was to win some for Christ and his Kingdom. The first characteristic the New Testament church displayed was that of *servanthood*. We must be willing to become servants in order to win some for Christ. The reason Paul was so effective in the small towns and rural areas in his day was that he behaved as a servant in order to work effectively with those receptive, in order to win them. He also worked hard as a servant among the resistant, so that when they became receptive he would be available to win them. Servanthood is a key to winning receptive people today, just as it was in the early church.

A second characteristic of the New Testament church comes also from Paul: the characteristic of *single-mindedness*. His single purpose was to know Christ and make him known.

> *His method for establishing a new congregation was to visit the synogogue on the Sabbath, where he was invited to speak. His message was of Jesus the Messiah, of the forgiveness of sins, of freedom from bondage of law, and of the "power of God for salvation . . ."*[11]

Paul was single-minded in his approach. "Paul's strategy for growth was to find and win responsive people . . . people whom God had prepared."[12]

The Bible tells of Paul going to Philippi and being unable to find a synagogue in which to preach. He went outside the city and found a prayer group. While there he baptized its leader, Lydia, and all her family.

> *Paul found receptive people and from there he used the existing "webs" of contacts which these new converts had to their friends and relatives; and from these new converts to other friends and relatives, and to others, and others.* [13]

Paul's single-minded goal was to reach and win the lost, and he gave his life for that purpose.

A third New Testament concept for reaching the receptive was that of *deliberate strategy.*

> *As we study the Scripture in more detail we see that the early church grew primarily through relationships between friends, family, servants, neighbors. Indeed, a solid case can be presented that Paul's strategy for establishing churches was, in large part, to find responsive people, convert them, and then reach others in the new converts' webs of relationships. Responsiveness was found as the gospel spread through the webs of family, friends, and associates.* [14]

Paul and his followers had a single-minded goal of winning receptive people to Christ. Using a straightforward manner of presenting the gospel to those who were receptive, they followed a strategy of holding lightly the resistant and vigorously evangelizing those who were receptive. The churches on the mission fields they started were growing churches. The Apostle Paul and the missionaries who followed him followed the leading of the Holy Spirit to win the lost. The Holy Spirit wanted them to be single-minded, straightforward and to use his strategy.

The leadership of the Holy Spirit is illustrated in the Macedonian-call in Acts 16:5-15. Paul, Silas and Timothy were establishing churches and these churches were increasing in number daily. (Acts 16:5) They were told by the Holy Spirit not to preach the Word in Asia. (Acts 16:6) "After they were come to Mysia, they assayed to go into Bithynia: but the Spirit suffered them not." (Acts 16:7) In Troas a vision was given to them. "And a vision appeared to Paul in the night; There stood a man of Macedonia, and prayed him saying, Come over into Macedonia, and help us." (Acts 16:9) "And after he had seen the vision, immediately we endeavoured to go into Macedonia, assuredly gathering that the Lord had called us for to preach the gospel unto them." (Acts 16:10)

The Holy Spirit led these three evangelists away from towns and regions which were resistant to towns and regions which were receptive. One might say that Lydia and her prayer group constituted a country church down along the river outside the city. They were ready to receive the full gospel and they received it gladly.

The churches Paul and his companions started were soon healthy, growing churches. Spiritual gifts are at work in churches that are growing. Growing churches are healthy because they are using the right mix. C. Peter Wagner says,

> *Only healthy bodies grow well, and only healthy churches grew well — it is one of the signs of good health. Statements such as, "Our church is losing members, but we are healthy," do not square with all the Biblical data as to what God expects from the Body of Christ. One of the healthy church models we have in the New Testament is the Jerusalem church following Pentecost. Among other signs of good health, the Lord was adding daily such as should be saved (see Acts 2:47). If the Lord is not regularly adding new members, something is wrong with the church.*[15]

Moreover, the church that is not growing is a church that is not following the leadership of the Holy Spirit in reaching the receptive people God wants it to reach. In our rural and small town communities today there are receptive people God has prepared for us. As we follow the Holy Spirit's leading, God will send these people to us; or, better yet, he will send us *to these people* for evangelization.

The time has come for small town and rural churches to stop their negative thinking about the resistance all around them and begin "launching out into the deep" (To borrow an image from Jesus as he taught Peter and the other disciples about fishing). Certainly fishing is difficult and there is the possibility of not catching anything. However, if we enthusiastically follow the leadership of the Holy Spirit, God can and will bless the little churches in the small towns and rural areas. There are receptive people in these areas. The small town and rural church can grow by reaching them.

The Apostle Peter (Luke 5) launched out into the deep as Jesus comanded. The result was an overwhelming number of fish. If we never "attempt the impossible," we will never have the marvelous experience of being part of "God's miracle business."

The fishermen were seeking fish prior to Jesus' command, but not catching any. Could it be that the fish they were searching for were *resistant* fish and that Jesus led them to *receptive* fish? Could it also be that we spend nights, weeks, months trying to reach resistant people even while there are receptive people right on the other side fo town or just on the next country road?

The church I formerly served was a growing church for many reasons. One was that we were appealing to the receptive people to whom God had led us. These people were open to the gospel message. They responded because we allowed ourselves to be led to them. However, there were many people in our community who were not being won to Christ because we had accepted them as resistant. Receptive people came to us because we were a responsive church which had enthusiasm. They were ripe to accept us and we took advantage of their responsiveness. The experience I had in that church is being repeated in other small town and rural churches across America. We need to accept the place into which God has placed us and believe that we, too, are in a mission field.

We can reach ordinary people in ordinary places. Consider Jesus. He was born of a peasant girl from Nazareth, engaged to a small-town carpenter.

The Son of God learned the carpenter's trade and carried heavy planks and beams on His head and shoulders. Like the masses everywhere, He ate His bread "in the sweat of his face."[16]

It was in Nazareth that Jesus announced his purpose for coming to us:

The Spirit of the Lord is upon me, because he has anointed me to preach good news to the poor. He has sent me to proclaim release to the captives and recovering of sight to the blind, to set at liberty those who are oppressed. (Luke 4:18)

The groups of people our Lord was going to reach were the receptive people in the land. They were the poor, the brokenhearted, the captives, the blind and the bruised. His emphasis was on those in need and those in need are those receptive to the gospel.

Those he later called to follow him were the small town and country people.

122

> *Of the twelve apostles, eleven were Galileans — country people who spoke with an accent. The rulers, elders, scribes, and high priests scorned them as "uneducated common men." The book of Acts tells us that the Christian religion spread through the masses in Jerusalem and Judea. The common people heard the apostles gladly. The rulers of the Jews were afraid to act against the apostles because they feared the people. "The people," we are told, held the apostles in high esteem and when the captain with officers went and brought the apostles (Acts 5:18) to the high priest, they did so without violence "for they were afraid of being stoned by the people." It is no wonder that the masses were solidly behind the Early Church. She was made up largely of the common people and had common people for leaders.[17]*

"Country folk who spoke with an accent" led the church of the first century to great heights for God. The "little people" from insignificant towns and rural areas influenced the masses of receptive people of their day. The results of their evangelizing are still being felt today.

Those who were receptive in the small towns influenced larger areas for Christ. The resistant Jewish leadership, entrenched in high esteem, rejected and scorned the gospel. Therefore, Jesus took the people of low esteem and used them to bring the gospel to the world. In our day God can use the people of small towns and rural areas to evangelize the masses. God can use the people of small towns and rural areas when they understand resistance and receptivity. As small towns and rural communities are evangelized, after the model of the first century church, Church Growth will occur!

Let's summarize.

1. *We must occupy resistant fields lightly.*

> *They will turn receptive some day. They also have children of God living in them. Their populations are made up of men and women for whom Christ died. While they continue in their rebellious and resistant state, they should be given the opportunity to hear the Gospel in as courteous a way as possible. But they should not be heavily occupied last, fearing that they will be swamped by Christians, they become ever more resistant.[18]*

In every small town and rural setting these resistant pockets exist. We need to hold them lightly until they become receptive. We need to spend our time and energy on the receptive until the reistant become receptive. "Reinforcing receptive areas is the only mode of mission by which resistant populations *which become receptive* may be led to responsible membership in ongoing churches of Christ."[19]

2. *We must approach highly-receptive groups with first-priority evangelism.* These pockets of receptive people need to be evangelized while they are receptive. Donald McGavran says of receptive people.

> *True, not every missionary is going to encounter a highly receptive population, but some of them will. No one can tell in advance who will and who will not. Every missionary, therefore, ought to have instruction in how churches may be planted among populations which show great response to the Gospel.*[20]

Moreover, rural and small town churches must know how to identify and reach receptive people. These receptives are in the communities of rural and small town America and they are ready to be reached. Let us identify them. Let us reach them!

3. *Small town and rural churches can grow if they are rooted in the New Testament perspective.* People today are looking to the word of God for answers in their lives. A biblically based approach of winning the lost will succeed. People today want biblcal preaching. The Bible-based approach is working in rural and small towns across America. It can work in all of our churches. It can work for your church.

In the concluding chapter we will consider how to develop Church Growth strategy for small town and rural churches.

Questions for Discussion of Chapter 7

1. How are resistant people identified?

2. What are some signs of receptive people?

3. How was the Apostle Paul aware of resistant and receptive people?

4. What is the Holy Spirit's role in resistance and receptivity?

5. Name some resistant groups in your rural settings. In your small town setting.

6. Who are the receptive in your rural area? In your small town?

Footnotes

[1]Donald A. McGavran, *Understanding Church Growth,* p. 216.

[2]*Ibid.,* p. 216.

[3]*Ibid.,* p. 216.

[4]*Ibid.,* p. 229.

[5]*Ibid.,* p. 230.

[6]C. Peter Wagner, *Your Spiritual Gifts Can Help You Church Grow* (Ventura, California: Regal Books, 1979) p. 172.

[7]Charles Arn, Win Arn and Donald McGavran, *Growth A New Vision For The Sunday School* (Pasadena: Church Growth Press, 1980) p. 76.

[8]*Ibid.,* p. 76.

[9]*Ibid.,* p. 76, quoting *Membership Trends: A Study of Decline and Growth in the United Methodist Church,* 1949-1975, p. 6.

[10]*Ibid.,* p. 80.

[11]Charles Arn, et al., *Growth A New Vision for the Sunday School,* pp. 71-72.

[12]*Ibid.,* p. 72.

[13]*Ibid.,* p. 72.

[14]*Ibid.,* p. 73, quoting *The Pastor's Church Growth Handbook,* p. 112.

[15]C. Peter Wagner, *Your Spiritual Gifts Can Help Your Church Grow,* p. 172.

[16]Donald McGavran, *Understanding Church Growth,* p. 245.

[17]*Ibid.,* p. 245.

[18]*Ibid.,* p. 230.

[19]*Ibid.,* p. 230.

[20]*Ibid.,* p. 230.

Chapter 8

How to Develop Church Growth Strategy for the Small Town and Rural Church

We are now at the crossroads of "Church Growth Highway" and "Go Along As Before Boulevard." If you, the reader of this book, make a decision to "go along as before" after reading this far, you might as well stop reading now. However, if you are ready to embark on the most exciting journey your church has ever traveled, continue with your reading, because you have chosen "Church Growth Highway."

We have discussed the pertinent Church Growth principles in the preceding chapters. Now the focus is on strategy. The strategy offered in this chapter can enable your small town or rural church to grow.

Permit me to share a graphic skit we often act out in each of our Church Growth seminars. In the seminar I appoint people from the group to come forward to act out the work of the local volunteer fire department. I assign a person to make the firemen's beds. Another person prepares the meals while someone else shines the fire pole for the firemen's quick departure. Still another person washes and shines the fire trucks. The last person I choose is to take the firehouse dog out for a walk.

After I have made the assignments, I instruct the rest of the group to observe while the actors and actresses pantomime their roles. Each one performs his or her assigned role for a few minutes before I pull my imaginary fire bell and give out a loud "Clang! Clang!" Standing at their "fire" assignments for a few moments, they wonder what to do. I thank them for their participation and ask them to return to their seats.

Then I ask the most important question, the one that begins to prepare them for real Church Growth thinking. "What is the job of the local volunteer fire department?"

The answer comes loud and clear: "The job of the local volunteer fire department is to put out fires, to help families in need, and to assist people when their house is on fire!"

My response is, "What, then, were our actors and actresses doing up front a moment ago?"

"Well," the group members decide, "They were doing maintenance, housekeeping tasks for the firemen, or just biding time."

Immediately I will change the group's whole train of thinking by asking, "What is the job of the local church?"

The answers start coming in, "To help people in need."

"To evangelize the lost," someone says.

"To start fires in people's lives," another says.

Yes, they have the job description of the local church. But then I ask, "What does the church usually find itself doing?"

The answers of the group's participants are: "Putting cushions on the pews."

"Having a cleaning day at the church building."

"Adding a new addition."

"Making plans for the church social."

"But," I break in, "What is the *work* of the local church?"

"To win the lost to Christ," someone answers.

By now the whole group is on the same wavelength, ready to deal with the work of the church and, we hope, to open the path for Church Growth strategy for the small town and rural church.

The Importance of a Church Growth Pastor

I have already pointed out the importance of a Church Growth pastor in an earlier chapter. C. Peter Wagner's book, *Your Church Can Grow,* lists the seven vital signs of a healthy church:

> *Vital Sign Number One of a healthy, growing church is a pastor, who is a possibility thinker and whose dynamic leadership has been used to catalyze the entire church into action for growth.* [1]

The first way a small town and rural church can develop a Church Growth Strategy is to realize the importance of their pastor. Whether you are part of the itinerate system or the call system, you must put first priority on the importance of obtaining the proper pastor for your church.

I hear complaints from small town and rural churches that when their pastor starts moving with a good program, he is transferred. The reason for his transfer is to provide a monetary promotion and a larger church. I really believe these complaining laymen have a point. If more of our small town and rural churches could retain their present ministers for five to ten more years, the chance of these churches growing would be enhanced. In the United Methodist Church, some of our annual conferences have four-year rules. These rules mean that after four years the minister must move. A few years ago, a friend of mine, in another conference came to a dying, small town church; that church under his dynamic leadership began to grow dramatically. But because of the four-year rule that minister was moved to another church, and those laymen were devastated and the minister was shocked. The importance of this minister staying in that turned-from-decline-to-new-growth church would — and should — far outweigh a four-year rule. The annual conference to which I am referring needs to change its policies.

My own United Methodist annual conference probably stresses moving far more than necessary. I am an example of what more than a four-year pastorate can do for a church. The church I served at Convoy, Ohio, did not begin to grow until I had been with it four years. In fact, the final eight plus years I served there made a vast difference. The Director of Evangelism and Stewardship of our Conference, Dr. Carl Ling, told our membership a few years ago that I would lead them boldly as a pastor because I had earned their respect. He was right. Long-term pastorates are important. For those readers who are in "call" churches, it is essential you provide incentives for your pastor to encourage and entice him or her to continue as a long-term pastor of your church. A pastor "who is a possibility thinker and whose dynamic leadership has been used to catalyze the entire church into action for growth" (Vital Sign Number One) is first of all a pastor who has earned trust and respect.

How can the pastor and the Pastor-Parish Relations Committee (or whatever a similar group in your church is called) work out more long-term pastorates? First of all, the pastor can decide when he moves to a church that it is going to be his only and last church and plan to spend his life there. Politics in the ministry tempt us to use church appointments to our personal advantage as stepping stones to higher appointments, instead of places to really work through the gospel and be committed to people for perhaps an entire generation. We need to re-evaluate. In my own case, I had "gotten itchy" to move many times because of the movement I saw among United Methodist clergy all around me. Yet, I thank God that he kept me in the church I recently served for over twelve years. Clearly that church and I would have not realized the real growth I had envisioned for the church unless had I served that as long as I actually did. The church I am presently serving also needs my long-term attention and commitment.

Secondly, the Pastor-Parish Committee needs to understand its job description more carefully. Many of our committees only meet when problems arise. If a Pastor-Parish Committee really carried out its task I am confident more ministers would stay longer in one church. Let's face it, if committee members would treat their ministers as though they were really concerned about them, and in turn promote them financially, and support them emotionally, they would not want to move. When another church is dangled temptingly before them, they will remember they are better off staying where they are.

Third, the conference judicatory leader needs to re-evaluate the tendency toward musical chairs in ministerial appointments. I have talked to ministers who were encouraged to move by higher-up leaders precisely when they were involved in very successful ministries. Thank God, a few of them turned down those move requests. Even while I say this, I recognize that there are circumstances making a pastoral move — even after a relatively short stay — imperative. Conference judicatory leaders must spend many agonizing hours, days, even months, in deliberation over pastoral appointments and placements. On balance, however, I believe the principle holds. I urge pastors, Pastor-Parish Committees, and conference judicatory leaders to seriously consider longer pastoral appointments and placements. I am confident such a policy will help churches grow.

C. Peter Wagner says that in America the pastor is the primary catalytic factor for growth.

You can check this out for yourself. Just take a book like Great Churches of Today *or Elmer Towns'* America's Fastest Growing Churches *and note the examples given of growing churches cited*

130

> *in these books. They have grown under the leadership of one per-*
> *son in particular to whom God has given special gifts and who is*
> *using these gifts to lead the church into growth.* [2]

The pastor should realize how important he or she is to the church. We pastors of small town and rural churches are not the executive heads of our churches like many of the super-church leaders and para-church leaders are to theirs. But we are the spiritual heads of our churches, and we have the Holy Spirit to guide us. The time has come for us to stand boldly in our small town and rural churches and lead our people along the way to Church Growth. As we build respect among our people, they will begin to trust our leadership.

> *As I visit growing church after growing church I try to get the pulse*
> *of the average person in the pew as far as his or her attitude toward*
> *the pastor is concerned. Invariably I find a high degree of love and*
> *esteem for him. As a matter of fact, this is often exaggerated to the*
> *extent that many members of a growing church will claim — and*
> *sincerely so — that their pastor is the best pastor in the whole world.* [3]

Clearly, a church that has respect and trust in its pastor can be a dynamically growing church. A dynamically growing church is the kind of church that has a dynamic leader who is a possibility thinker.

Another of C. Peter Wagner's books, *Your Spiritual Gifts Can Help Your Church Grow* sounds a clarion call to dynamic pastoral leadership. In his chapter five, "The Pastor and His Gift-Mix," Wagner says,

> *As far as the growth of the local church is concerned . . . the pastor*
> *is the key individual. The pastor, of course, is not the only factor*
> *for growth in a local church, but he is probably the most important*
> *one.* [4]

Dr. Wagner admits that stressing the importance of the pastor for Church Growth has caused criticism; yet he still holds to his view that strong dynamic pastors can lead a church to growth.

He alludes to studies made by several denominations, including the author's own United Methodist Church, concerning the concept of pastoral leadership in Church Growth.

*The Methodist study, for example, speaks of the several organiza-
tions now studying church growth: "In one way or another, they
all recognize the pastor is the key person. They may disagree about
how the pastor should be involved but they all agree that the pastor
must be involved." There are many reasons for this, but the study
highlights one of them arguing that "the pastor's involvement sig-
nals his or her commitment to the conviction that one of the most
important tasks of the local congregation is that of extending the
ministry of the church to include more persons."[5]*

For those who are pastors of the United Methodist Church, there
is understandable apprehension at this point. We United Methodist
pastors know that Pastor-Parish Committee members and the District Superintendent already know that our churches rise or fall because of our leadership. We already know it, so let us accept it. The
time has come for ministers to accept responsibility and begin plow-
ing forward toward the harvest of Church Growth. We, the *leaders*
of our churches, no matter what our denominational affiliation, are
responsible for our churches' futures. Our small town and rural
churches need our leadership in order to grow.

Dr. Wagner anticipates the negative feedback sure to come:

*While some resistance to this may be due to humility, probably much
more is due to a reluctance on the part of many pastors to shoulder
so much responsibility. In neither case are the objections adequate.
Church people in general are coming to realize more than ever before that if a person accepts the responsibility of being the pastor
of a church, he accepts the primary responsibility for its growth or
decline just as much as an airplane pilot accepts responsibility for
keeping his plane in the air. It won't fly without wings and stabilizer
and engine, true. But recognizing that doesn't change the fact that
the pilot is the one who makes it fly.[6]*

Jesus is the head of the Church universal, but he directs his chosen
pastors to lead his churches. The pastor's duty, then, is to follow
Christ's leading as he directs and leads the church.

In the small town and rural church there are three commitments
that a Church Growth pastor should make:

• First, he or she is called by God to lead his or her congregation into Church Growth. He or she must commit himself or herself
to this call, using all the abilities he or she has through the gifts and
graces God has given him or her.

- Second, he or she will commit himself or herself to stay in his or her appointment until he or she has established respect and trust from the congregation, and the church has grown in numbers, membership, attendance in celebration services and attendance in Sunday school.
- Third, he or she must be willing to pay the price of growth which could mean lower salary and pastoral esteem for being in a small town or rural church where judicatory or national recognition might not be given.

I am convinced that many of our small town and rural churches will grow when a large number of pastors make this threefold commitment. The choice is ours as pastors. The result will be growing, dynamic denominations in which small town and rural pastors will have led the way. Having begun to start fires in people to bring them alive with a new spark in the soul, we will have demonstrated the importance of being Church Growth pastors.

The Importance of an Inspired Laity for Growth

The importance of an inspired laity for Church Growth cannot be underestimated. As a pastor I have just laid down the law for my fellow pastors. I have given them the truth and the truth means work — *hard* work. Lay persons, perhaps, have cheered my comments and said "Amen" to what they have just read. But now it is the laymen and the laywomen's turn to take a long, hard look in the ecclesiastical mirror.

Rise up, laymen and laywomen. It is time to stand up and be counted. An inspired laity is of supreme importance to a growing church. In order for a church to grow, it takes many hours of hard work by sometimes countless people. The unsung heros of the church that is growing are legion. However, the key is not their hard work but rather the inspiration which has led them into that hard work. The enthusiasm of an inspired laity will rub off upon a whole community. People outside the church will sense this enthusiasm, and it will rub off on community affairs and deliberations. Other churches of the community will also be touched by it. New people will come to the church because they want to be a part of an inspired and enthusiastic church. And the church will grow.

The method of the church since its inception in the first century has been that of gathering and then scattering. This method is spelled out in the book of Acts.

*Christians have always been a "gathering people," finding comfort
and strength in God and in one another as they met for thanksgiv-
ing, adoration, instruction, and inspiration.*[7]

It is important that a church gathers to grow together.

The church then goes out or scatters to share what it has heard
enthusiastically.

*We also find the early congregations were a "scattering church."
The early Christians were continually spreading the good news of
the gospel in the temple, in their homes, and in the streets. (Acts
5:28, 42)*[8]

The value of an inspired laity for growth is demonstrated in the
response of that laity when called upon to lead. They enthusiastically accept authority to carry out the task of the church. When the
church is gathered, they are visible in their leadership rules. When
the church is scattered, the results of their leadership make an imprint upon the community at large.

How then are the laity inspired for growth? The answer to that
question is found in the call of the Great Commission. Christ called
us to obedience to that commission. We are to go out and multiply
the church through ministering to the needs of hurting people. Obedience to the call to evangelize as the body of Christ is not our duty
but our privilege as those who have been redeemed.

*We accept the commission as a privilege, to join him in the Way
he is leading. Churches that accept this offered privilege and have
their priorities straight are free to experience apostolic growth.*[9]

A Church Growth pastor commands trust and respect. Consequently,
he or she can unashamedly call the church to the privilege of
obedience to the Great Commission.

In fact, the call to obedience is heard not only in the Great Commission. It runs through the entirety of both the Old and the New
Testaments. That message of obedience is the root of the gospel.
The obedient are the truly self-fulfilled. The obedient are truly the
happy. The obedient are truly the successful. Can we say also the
obedient are the churches that are growing in numbers? I believe

we can.

The critics of number-counting each Sunday might say, "We are to be faithful, not successful." But the first century church, our model, was not merely faithful; it was a growing, dynamic church. Numbers were counted and discussed. We are to inspire our laity to be obedient and, in turn, through their obedience to the Great Commission they will become inspired and the church will grow.

In every small town and rural church I have visited for Church Growth seminars, I have found a small nucleus of inspired laity. The pastors of those churches already had in them a group to make the church come alive.

I have heard from these inspired laity some positive comments which seemed to be common to all of them.

• First, they believe the gospel stories to be true and applicable to today's church. The Bible is real to these leaders, and they are willing to test the gospel truths to their own local church.

• Second, they are willing to apply any abilities they have to see their church grow. Many of them do not understand the gifts of the Spirit. Because of their lack of understanding of the gifts, they have not discovered their own personal gifts. Excitement is high when they come to understand that they have one or more spiritual gifts and are also immediately able to identify gifts in their fellow believers. They leave our seminars determined to use these gifts that they have just discovered.

• Third, they want to hear new ideas about how their church can grow; such sharing has made these seminars very exciting. For example, when I mentioned to one church the idea of taking families out to dinner in order to win them to Christ and his church, one layman immediately caught on to the idea which is used by the secular world to win clients. He said he would be willing to spend $50.00 on a family for a night out just to become better acquainted and possibly win them to Christ.

• Fourth, lay persons in small town and rural churches where I have been believe their churches *can* grow. These laymen and laywomen *believe* in their churches. They are willing to work hard for what they believe.

With people who believe the gospel stories to be true, people who are willing to apply any abilities they have, people who want to hear new ideas, and people who believe their church can grow, I am convinced we have the basis for Church Growth.

With these willing and believing leaders and God's Holy Spirit to guide, we have found in the inspired laity a way to develop Church Growth strategy. Our small town and rural churches can grow because we have the right kind of laity ready to turn our churches around. An inspired laity with a Church Growth pastor as spiritual leader can be the basis for making our churches grow.

The Importance of the Gift of Evangelist

I would like to stress the great importance of the gift of evangelist to the way of developing Church Growth strategy for small town and rural churches.

Equal in importance to the Church Growth pastor and an inspired laity, is that of the gift of evangelist. This gift is of primary significance to Church Growth.

In order to understand the gift of evangelist, it is necessary first to consider the concept of spiritual gifts. While several outstanding books are available on the subject of spiritual gifts, a few words on the subject in general is appropriate here.

> *"I would not have you ignorant" (of spiritual gifts) are the inspired words of the apostle Paul in 1 Corinthians 12:1. The church in Corinth that Paul was writing to desperately needed instruction on spiritual gifts.* [10]

In like manner does the small town and rural church need instruction concerning spiritual gifts. I am convinced that if every leader of small town and rural churches would discover, develop and use his or her spiritual gifts those churches would come alive.

Spiritual gifts are the special abilities given by God to carry out his work in and through the church. "A spiritual gift is a special attribute given by the Holy Spirit to every member of the Body of Christ according to God's grace for use within the context of the body." [11] Spiritual gifts are given to Christians to use within the context of the church and for use by the church to reach out to those outside the body of Christ.

> *Not everybody has spiritual gifts. Unbelievers do not. But every Christian person who is committed to Jesus and truly a member of His Body has at least one gift, or possibly more. The Bible says that*

every Christian has received a gift (see 1 Peter 4:10), and that "the manifestation of the Spirit is given to every man to profit" (1 Corinthians 12:7).[12]

Each Christian needs to discover his or her gift or gifts in order to properly use them for the body of Christ. The gift of evangelist is one of the most important primary gifts God uses to win the lost and grow the church. C. Peter Wagner stresses that as the reproductive organs are of primary importance in the human body so the reproductive organ of the body Christ is of primary importance.

The gift of evangelist is the primary organ that God has provided for reproduction. But the finest gift of evangelist in Christendom will not help churches to grow if the other members of the Body, the secondary organs for church growth, are not also functioning in a healthy manner.[13]

A marriage relationship can reproduce a child biologically but if this marriage relationship becomes unhealthy, then the child can grow up confused and distraught with life. The same can be said of an unhealthy church (or body of Christ) which can beget confused and distraught converts.

It is important to remember, then, that the gift of evangilist works hand in hand with the other gifts to bring glory to God through the church.

The gift of evangelist is the special ability that God gives to certain members of the Body of Christ to share the gospel with unbelievers in such a way that men and women become Jesus' disciples and responsible members of the Body of Christ.[14]

Those who have the gift of evangelist have discovered it as others have discovered their spiritual gifts. "The process of discovering this gift is the same as that for any other. Experiment, examine your feelings, evaluate your effectiveness, and expect confirmation from the Body."[15]

Those with the gift of evangelist use the gift by going to lost people and persuading them to make a profession of Jesus Christ as Savior.

Permit an example from my own life. God's called upon me to preach. In that call he made it very clear he wanted me to be an evangelist. Because my call was so real, I was certain I was called to be another Billy Graham.

Later, when God did not lead me into full-time evangelism, but instead, gave me the desire to become an evangelistic pastor with only occasional evangelistic meetings, I began to see my calling *not* as mass evangelism but instead as *pastoral* evangelism.

Later, when I became involved with the Church Growth movement, I truly began to understand evangelism. Prior to my understanding of evangelism from the Church Growth movement, I used to believe we were all called to evangelize our neighbors. Those who were not evangelizing were, I thought, inferior Christians. Then the Church Growth leaders taught me that evangelism was a gift that only *some* in the Body of Christ had. Instead of all Christians evangelizing, I now understood that all Christians were called *to witness their faith*. To witness is to let your life so shine before men that they may see Christ in you. A witness is to let his or her light shine in thought, word and deed every day.

I used to think that to be an evangelist was to be like Billy Graham. Now I know that Billy Graham is *one type* of evangelist, the mass evangelist. There is another type of evangelist: the one given to one-on-one evangelism. Some who have this gift can be either mass evangelists or one-on-one evangelists. My calling began to fit in with my ministry when I saw this definition of the gift of evangelist. I had the gift of both personal and mass evangelism, but God had called me to use my gift as a pastoral evangelist.

Church Growth leaders informed me that studies have demonstrated that approximately ten percent of a typical church in America had the gift of evangelist.

> *A mounting quantity of empirical evidence indicates that if a church has ten percent, or even a few percentage points less than ten percent, of its active members mobilized for evangelism, a growth pattern of two hundred percent per decade is a realistic expectation. If God blesses a church by giving the gift of evangelism to more than ten percent of its members, it is in wonderful shape for growth.*[16]

The ideal way to use the ten percent with the gift of evangelist is to send them out, teamed with "brand new" converts, to win the friends and associates of the new converts. The web evangelism effect which results from this type of evangelism wins many friends of the new convert of Christ.

Through my research with small town and rural churches, I have found this ten percent rule to be true. In the Church Growth seminars, the members of the group have been able to identify those with the gift of evangelist. Immediately we are able to inspire those with the gift to begin making implementation of that gift for winning the lost through the church structure. This, of course, is part of the way to develop Church Growth strategy. The gift of evangelism is of primary importance for strategy development.

In my former church in Convoy, Ohio, we sent out our evangelists two-by-two each week to witness to those who were receptive and to bring them into the body of Christ through salvation and church membership. This methodical, week by week procedure produced lasting results in our church. It can also produce lasting results in your church. Those with the gift of evangelism must be identified and then urged to use their gift for your local church. I believe that every small town and rural church has enthusiastic lay persons who are willing to discover and develop the gift. They will use the gift when they realize they have it and understand its use. "It could be just what your church needs to get the message to the unsaved, bring new believers into your fellowship and begin an exciting era of growth to the glory of God."[17]

The Implementation of the Calling Program

The implementation of the calling program is another vital part of the way to develop Church Growth strategy for the small town and rural church. Even when all other strategy is working toward Church Growth, the actual implementation of the calling program is still the needed ingredient. Without an effective calling program, which includes the use of the gift of evangelist through inspired laity, a church cannot sustain a long term positive growth pattern.

The calling program capitalizes on the gift of evangelist. However, not everyone in a calling program of a local church needs to have the gift of evangelist. Only about fifty percent of those involved in the calling program need the gift of evangelist.

In order to begin a calling program in a local church, the membership must, first, understand what a calling program is and, second, how it functions in the strategy of Church Growth.

What, then, is a calling program in the local church? A calling program is a regular, deliberate, planned program of visitation within the immediate and surrounding community of the local church. This planned program includes persons who have been trained by the pastor or other designated professionals in the attitudes and attributes of personal house-to-house visitation. Each visitor must know the social graces involved and have a sense of spiritual insight about people and their need for personal commitment to Christ. The program is a regular week-by-week commitment by the trained visitors. It usually involves an afternoon or evening each week.

A calling program, along with invitations to discipleship in worship services and smaller groups, is part of the total evangelism of the church. By going house-to-house the callers are impressing upon those on whom they call, and upon the whole community, that theirs is a caring church. In American culture people expect ministers to go door-to-door in a community, but when two laymen come in the name of Christ, the ones being visited realize that the visit is unusual. The calling program needs to be divided into categories of houses to be visited, and then assigned in terms of who makes which type of visit.

There are five basic types of home visits:

- 1. *Those who are new in the community.* All new people in the community need to be welcomed by the church. I call this call "the welcome wagon call." The visit is short and to the point. The callers identify who they are and the church they represent. They introduce the church by giving the new people a packet of introduction. The packet I have developed includes names of other community churches and their pastors. It also includes a tract type booklet or two. The callers also give them a list of school programs and administrative personnel and two names of baby sitters they recommend if they have children. Sometimes a plate of cookies or cakes have been taken. The visit is a welcome and an introduction to the church. If the visitors feel the family seems interested in the church, they indicate so on the calling form. (The form and its contents will be clarified later.)

- 2. *Those who have visited the church for Sunday worship.* This call is made during that week after the visit to the church. Some authorities on calling say it should be made within twenty-four hours of the church visit. I would say within seventy-two hours would be adequate. The callers from the church let the visitors know how glad they were to have them in their church. The callers find out from them information about their family to record on a calling card. By asking simple leading questions, the callers discover whether they are further interested in the church.

- 3. *Those who are inactive members of the church.* (John Savage has developed an entire program of reaching the inactive in the church.) The callers need to make these people aware that they care about them and have missed them in church. They listen to them and can find out by listening for clues as to why they stopped going to church.

- 4. *The shut-ins.* This visit is needed to let the shut-ins know the church cares and is interested in them. Usually a caller can discover from them those ministries with which the church can assist them.

- 5. *Evangelism calls.* These calls comes from the results of all the other calls or from experiences the church has with people who are in need for evangelism and have a receptivity for the gospel.

What are the categories of callers who make these calls? There are basically two groups. We could call one group the *regular callers* and the other group the *evangelists.*

1. *Regular Callers.* These people are trained to make a simple courteous visit. They can call on the new people in the community ("welcome wagcon" calls), those who visit the worship service, and the shut-ins. A person does not have to have the gift of evangelist to make any of these calls. The person only needs to be a good listener and be willing to give time to go out and meet people.

2. *The evangelists.* Those with the gift of evangelist have already been identified in this chapter. They are qualified to make calls on inactive members and evangelism calls.

The calling program can bring rewarding results to a church when it is prayerfully placed in high esteem by the membership of the church. In my former pastorate we had a successful calling program for over nine years. We reserved three hours every Tuesday night for our calling time. We began by gathering in the pastor's study at the designated hour, where assignments were received. Each of us offered a prayer, and we then went out, two-by-two. The chairman of our calling program and I made the assignments. At the end of the evening we returned to report to the group both our successes and our disappointments. This sharing or reporting at the end was helpful because on any given night one calling team might not have had much success and those with successes would encourage them. The only group that is careful in the report back session is the evangelist group, since they will properly have determined to keep some calls confidential. We finished the evening by sharing prayer sentences from all our callers.

In those nine years we brought into membership each year an average of seventeen percent of those who visited the church. New people in the community had given us a ten percent return. Ten percent of the inactive became active again and forty percent more of them returned to worship two or three times because of the visit. This was significant, even though we were not able to reactivate them.

We also averaged a ten percent conversion rate on all evangelism calls. We did not have all the answers, nor did we feel our methods were foolproof. However, they worked for us and I am confident that as you use these methods and modify them to fit your local church, you too will have success in winning people to Christ. I have already begun their implementation in my new pastorate.

We send our callers out two-by-two and we find it is best to send two men together and two women together. However, a man and wife combination can work. The important thing is to let the Lord guide in the selection and formation of the calling teams.

A final word on our calling program is in order. You will need to formulate a calling file. Each sheet in that file should include names of family members, address, phone, occupation of adult members, church affiliation, interests, their interest in your church and who called. There should be room on the sheet for several calls. Each pastor can formulate his or her own calling file which will fit his or her situation.

Many churches have started calling programs only to have them fall by the wayside after a short period. To sustain a program of this importance and magnitude, it takes persistence and commitment by the church leaders and by those chosen to lead the program. I can report with great pride that every Tuesday night we went out calling in Convoy — rain or shine, snow or heat wave — for over nine years. However, I want to stress that we were only able to accomplish a program of this magnitude and importance with much prayer and persistence. The very first night we began our calling program, two of our original callers upon returning to the church announced they were ready to quit. They had gone to a home in which the beloved family Great Dane had slipped through the door as they were being invited in. The dog immediately ran into the street, was struck by a car and instantly killed. Our callers felt that it was their fault. If they had not knocked on the door, the dog would not have run out. I might add that one of the two callers to that home on that fateful first night continued as a faithful caller through the nine years I served there.

I must admit that the dynamic chairman who helped start the program, and faithfully encouraged other callers, left the church after two and one-half years. Furthermore, another chairman became discouraged with the task and suspended his calling indefinitely. Added to that disappointment, his wife also quit.

I can mention these defeats and rejoice. I know we had these difficulties because the enemy knew our program was reaching the lost. I rejoiced that he was trying to break down our program because then I knew it was succeeding. I knew God would overcome the devil and our program would continue.

I share these defeats to keep things in perspective. It is not easy to instigate a calling program. I share these defeats so that others will know that in the face of defeat there is victory.

Small churches will have a limited number of people to involve, but do not let this defeat you. A few dedicated callers can turn a small church into a much larger church. Be determined to try it and I guarantee that it will work.

Of critical importance, then, for implementing Church Growth are: Growth pastor, the inspired laity, and the gift of evangelist. The implementation of a calling program depends upon the presence of all three. These elements together can begin the process of Church Growth. All three, undergirded by the principles of Church Growth which have been discussed in the earlier chapters of this book, can make a small town or rural church grow. These principles can mix together with a church's spiritual gifts to make it a growing, vibrant community where people want to come and worship God.

> *Many people will not become Christians unless and until your church and hundreds of other churches like yours take seriously the command of Christ to make disciples of all nations. You and your church can participate in the harvest. You can win people to Christ and bring them into responsible church membership.*[18]

There are people in our rural and small town communities that are receptive to the gospel message. Our task, then, is to develop a strategy to reach these people and bring our churches to growth. The time has come for us to show our memberships that we are sincere about the gospel mandate to win the lost.

Small town and rural churches will grow when they are challenged to grow. The information in this book can be instrumental in making those churches grow. The larger churches in these small town and rural communities are already large in size and numbers because of progressive growth in the past. These larger churches can grow once again. If they are on a plateau, they can apply Church Growth principles and they will begin growing again. If these larger churches are declining, they can stop the decline and once again become growing, vibrant churches.

On the other hand the smaller churches in the small town and rural communities can grow as well. Carl S. Dudley says:

> *Rapid membership growth is possible for many small churches. A substantial minority of small churches could double their membership in the next few years. Rapid membership growth depends less on community potential, more on the values and attitudes of church members. Members of the congregation must want to grow so much that they are willing to give up the satisfactions of knowing, or knowing about, everyone else in the congregation. They must sacrifice the satisfactions of being a small church.*[19]

They must be willing to sacrifice the intimacy of the fellowship in the small church in order to reach new people and evangelize them. A small church leadership might agree to make these sacrifices and put their minds together for strategy for growth, only to find their hearts were not in the process. For this reason, the leadership must

144

change their minds as well as their hearts in order to grow.

> *When the community has growth potential, any congregation can grow — if the members are willing to let go of their satisfactions in being close to one another. Some small churches are "converted" to larger congregations, with a full program and something for everyone. But they are not small churches anymore.* [20]

Yes, Church Growth works for the small town and rural church. It worked for me in my ministry in Convoy, Ohio. I expect to see it work at the Wheelersburg, Ohio, church which I am now serving. It can work for you.

Get ready . . . Get set. . . Grow!

Questions for Discussion of Chapter 8

1. In your own words explain why a Church Growth pastor is so important for church growth.

2. Does your church have an inspired laity for growth? If so, list some of the reasons why.

3. What is the gift of evangelist and who in your group has it?

4. List the steps for setting up a calling program in your church.

5. How can your church develop a Church Growth strategy?

Footnotes

[1]C. Peter Wagner, *Your Church Can Grow,* p. 57.

[2]*Ibid.,* p. 55.

[3]*Ibid.,* p. 57.

[4]C. Peter Wagner, *Your Spiritual Gifts Can Help Your Church Grow,* pp. 137-138.

[5]*Ibid.,* p. 138, quoting *Membership Trends, A Study of Decline and Growth in the United Methodist Church,* 1949-1975, p. 19.

[6]*Ibid.,* pp. 140-141.

[7]Paul Benjamin, *The Growing Congregation,* p. 14.

[8]*Ibid.,* p. 14.

[9]George Hunter and Donald McGavran, *Church Growth Strategies That Work,* p. 14.

[10]C. Peter Wagner, *Your Spiritual Gifts Can Help Your Church Grow,* p. 31.

[11]*Ibid.,* p. 42.

[12]*Ibid.,* pp. 39-40.

[13]*Ibid.,* p. 172:

[14]*Ibid.,* p. 173.

[15]*Ibid.,* p. 173.

[16]*Ibid.,* p. 177.

[17]*Ibid.,* pp. 192-193.

[18]C. Peter Wagner, *Your Church Can Grow,* p. 170.

[19]Carl S. Dudley, *Making the Small Church Effective,* (Nashville: Abingdon, 1978), p. 51.

[20]*Ibid.,* p. 54.

Growth Chart

Convoy, Ohio, United Methodist Church

Year	Communicant Membership at Conclusion of Each Year	Average Sunday Morning Worship Attendance (52 Sundays)	Average Sunday Church School Attendance (52 Weeks)	Composite Membership Yearly Average
1969	372	171	155	233
1970	378	161	114	218
1971	384	151	114	216
1972	395	147	111	218
1973	369	145	105	206
1974	379	171	77	209
1975	378	167	70	205
1976	394	155	79	208
1977	398	160	67	208
1978	430	175	92	232
1979	439	181	94	238
1980	449	192	105	249
1981	472	192	106	257
1982	488	215	118	274
1983	510	220	122	284
1984	520	218	131	290

Bibliography

Arn, Charles, Win Arn and Donald McGavran. *Growth A New Vision For The Sunday School.* Pasadena: Church Growth Press, 1980.

Benjamin, Paul. *The Growing Congregation.* Lincoln, Ill.: Lincoln Christian College Press, 1972.

Boer, Harry R. *Pentecost and Missions.* Cambridge, England; Lutterworth Press, 1961.

Burtner, Robert W. and Chiles, Robert E. *A Compend of Wesley's Theology.* New York: Abingdon Press, 1954.

Dayton, Edward R. and Fraser, David A. *Planning Strategies For World Evangelization.* Grand Rapids: Eerdmans, 1980.

DeRidder, Richard R. *Discipling the Nations.* Grand Rapids: Baker, 1971.

Dudley, Carl S. *Making The Small Church Effective.* Nashville: Abingdon, 1978.

Glasser, Arthur F., Paul G. Hiebert, C. Peter Wagner and Ralph D. Winter. *Crucial Dimensions in World Evangelism.* Pasadena: William Carey Library, 1976.

Green, Michael. *Evangelism in the Early Church.* Kent, Hodder and Stoughton, 1970.

Hoge, Dean R. *A Test of Theories of Denominational Growth and Decline.* Chapter eight of *Understanding Church Growth and Decline 1950-1978.* Edited by Dean R. Hoge and David A. Roozen. New York: The Pilgrim Press, 1979.

Hunter, George G. III, McGavran, Donald. *Church Growth Strategies that Work.* Nashville: Abingdon, 1980.

(The) Journal of John Wesley. Percy Livingston Parker, ed. Chicago: Moody Press, n.d.

Kelley, Dean M. *Why Conservative Churches Are Growing.* New York: Harper and Row, 1972.

148

Komminga, Carol G. *Bringing God's News to Neighbors,* Nutley, N. J.: Presbyterian and Reformed, 1976.

Ladd, George E. *The Gospel of the Kingdom.* Exeter, Devon: The Paternoster Press Ltd, Paternoster House, 1975.

Mavis, W. Curry. *Advancing the Smaller Church.* Grand Rapids: Baker, 1968.

McGavran, Donald A. *Ethnic Realities and the Church: Lessons from India.* Pasadena: W. Carey Library, 1979.

_____. *Understanding Church Growth.* Grand Rapids: Eerdmans, 1970.

Snyder, Howard. *The Radical Wesley.* Downers Grove, Ill.: Intervarsity Press, 1980.

Sweet, William W. *Methodism in American History.* New York: Abingdon Press, 1953.

Wagner, C. Peter. *Our Kind of People.* Atlanta: John Knox Press, 1979.

_____. *Your Church Can Grow.* Glendale, California: Regal, 1976.

_____. *Your Spiritual Gifts Can Help Your Church Grow.* Ventura, California: Regal, 1979.

Wesley, John. *A Plain Account of Christian Perfection.* London: The Epworth Press, 1952.

Yoder, John. *Church Growth Issues In Theological Perspective,* Chapter II of *The Challenge of Church Growth — A Symposium.* Edited by Wilbert R. Shenk. Scottdale, Pa.: Herald Press, 1973.